"Is it realistic to be concerned with business succession when you have a young business or are just starting a business? ABSOLUTELY!! Janise Graham has presented a very concise step-by-step plan for anyone to follow and accomplish. This is a must-read for everyone in business as well as CPAs, Attorneys, Bankers, and entrepreneurs thinking of starting one."

> **CC Vest,** Former Co-owner and President of Midpoint
> Bearing. Established 1985. Left "In Style" 2021

"No one likes to think about the end game for their business. Why would we? And yet, without knowing where you are going, it's hard to carve out a meaningful journey along the way. Janise's ability to make the complicated simple makes *Leaving In Style* a must-read book for every business owner. If, God forbid, something happens to you or your business partner, what will happen to your family AND all of your employees who depend on you? Creating an exit strategy allows you to have peace of mind; and through story and strategy, Janise shows you exactly how to do that."

> **Ursula Mentjes,** 5x Bestselling Author
> and CEO of Ursula, Inc.

"Leaving In Style is full of wisdom, insight, and useful tips to help all business owners put good business practices 'in place just in case they don't make it back to work either temporarily or permanently.' Introducing Grace as an archetype, adding a bit of 'levity and fun to this challenging topic,' and sharing this information in story form made it very relatable, as well as easy to read and comprehend."

Janet Steiner, Former President and
CEO of Thoro Packaging
President of MakeDust
Founder of TradeWorksUSA

"In *Leaving In Style,* Janise tells an enlightening story of Grace and her journey with the intention of teaching each of us lessons in the importance of business succession. Janise's eloquent style of mentoring puts us in Grace's shoes with easy-to-understand lessons of the processes involved in the many aspects of business succession planning. There are so many 'aha' moments, as it reads like a novel, and I couldn't wait for what Janise was going to guide Grace with next. The fashion metaphor was an eloquent touch for the framework of the process and an added lesson for us women to always dress for confidence and success. Brilliant!"

Dian Wyman, Managing Partner, *Wyman & Little Inc.*
Accounting & Consulting

"This book takes you on a journey into business succession planning that is so easy to understand. The idea of putting a plan in place becomes a 'no-brainer.' This book will be very useful to new and seasoned business owners alike and should be suggested reading in educational courses."

Tammi Phillips, Former Business Owner

"I've been directly involved with three family businesses over my career and all three had the same conclusion: The owners didn't understand how to get out of their own business. Unfortunately, they didn't have Janise Graham's comprehensive and easy-to- understand guide to take them through the process of *'Leaving In Style.'* Janise has skillfully created the essential exit strategy tutorial for anyone operating their own business."

Ernie Silvers, MBA
Professor of Business and Entrepreneurship
Jack H. Brown College, School of Entrepreneurship

"Leaving In Style is wonderful storytelling combined with business strategies that Janise makes easy to understand. This is a very good book to gift a client or prospective client that needs to have a 'planning map.'"

Mike Ables, Mike Ables Insurance Services

"If you have said, 'I am going to get around to it,' and you look at the calendar like I did, and it is 15 years later, this book will make you gasp and then propel you into action. Paula's story could be my story or yours. If you treasure your family, your employees, and you, Janise engages us to act today! I have personally signed loan documents to fund almost $1 billion in loans for small business owners, and I can tell you this book is your roadmap, without excuse, to *Leave in Style*."

Hilda Kennedy, Founder President,
AmPac Business Capital

"*Leaving In Style* is thought-provoking and will cause you to rethink everything you thought about your retirement or business exit plan. I thought I had a great business exit plan. However, Grace's story introduced me to the importance of succession planning, a term I had not considered. Janise so eloquently tells the story of Grace and her sister, Paula, all while educating you on the importance of succession planning and having a plan for the unexpected. This book could not be more timely... It shows what could happen to your family and employees if you don't have a succession plan in place for your business."

Patricia Summers, Owner of California Smog &
Automotive Institute

"This is a great read. It is a documented fact that we learn best from experience and relatable storylines. This is that—sharing great insight, wisdom, and methods to inspire thought-provoking questions, strategies, and actions necessary for *Leaving In Style.* Why leave something so important to chance?"

Mark Maes, Principle at Maes and Associates, Architect of High Five Priority Business Mapping™

LEAVING
in Style

BUSINESS SUCCESS{ION}
ON YOUR TERMS

JANISE GRAHAM

Leaving In Style
Business Succession on Your Terms

Published by

Small Business Style, Inc.
Corona, CA
www.LeavingInStyle.com

Copyright © 2022 *by Small Business Style Inc.*

Cover & Interior Illustrations by Saima Latif
Cover Design by Dan Mulhern, Dan Mulhern Design Co.
Interior Design by Dawn Teagarden
Headshot by Ty Freeman

ISBN: 979-8-9859501-0-6

Printed in the United States of America

www.LeavingInStyle.com

To my husband Larry, for your unconditional and unwavering support and encouragement.

CONTENTS

13

Prologue

Leading and Leaving Gracefully

33

Introduction

Design Your Plan and Create Peace of Mind

43

Chapter One

Clarify Your WHY

59

Chapter Two

Identify Your Personal Style of Business Leadership

73

Chapter Three

Tailor Your Systems for Growth

89

Chapter Four

Create Confidence with Composure

125

Chapter Five

Step In Style Through the Transition

149

Chapter Six

Accessorize with a Dynamic Team of Experts

177

Chapter Seven

Reflect and Refine with Annual Reviews

193

Conclusion

Ready to Leave in Style?

199

About

Janise Graham

201

A Special

Invitation

203

Supporting

Women in Business

205

Acknowledgments

Prologue

LEADING AND LEAVING GRACEFULLY

GRACE DROVE SLOWLY past the guard station and towards the valet right in front of the Boca Raton Resort and Club. The energetic parking attendant greeted her warmly as he had for the past five years. The simple thought of this place made her smile, and she intuitively began to relax. Each year, Grace faithfully attended the Folding Carton Manufacturers Conference and was always delighted to get caught up with her industry friends from all over the world. They would converge, converse, and laugh over gourmet meals and her favorite key lime tarts. She was optimistic that this year would be like the rest since she had always left with a warmed heart and three or four great business ideas and insights. The colorful stories of family and business and customers always brought a peer mentoring aspect second to none.

"Can I help you with your luggage, Ms. Tena?" the valet asked as he opened her door.

"No, thank you so much. I think I can handle it from here." She smiled at the helpful young man.

After a deep sigh, Grace mustered up some energy, stepped out of her car, reached into the back seat, grabbed her computer bag and luggage with both hands, and headed towards the "BOCA pink" pink hotel with a sense of belonging.

"I'd prefer a room overlooking the lake, please." She smiled at the young lady behind the front desk. Grace always preferred staying in the Cloister building—the original section of this historic luxury hotel. The rooms had spacious balconies that overlooked some of the most scenic and picturesque views in Florida.

"Certainly, Ms. Tena. I think I have a room that you will like," she confidently replied.

"Oh, thank you so much," Grace said.

"My pleasure. It is good to see you again this year."

"It's terrific to be back here. I'm looking forward to relaxing. Thank you for this," Grace said as she grabbed her hotel key card and walked toward the elevator.

I can't wait to get to my room to collapse for a quick nap, Grace thought as she walked the long corridor to her room.

As she walked into her room and toward the mirror, she gasped at the reflection staring back at her. Her tall willowy frame appeared gaunt and fragile. The humidity added frizz to withered shoulder-length natural curls. She moved in for a closer look at her face that now seemed dulled and stressed. There were dark circles under her eyes and new wrinkles that had appeared overnight. Or at least it felt that way.

Look at me! I look 10 years older.

Grace was always impeccably dressed and delighted that she looked five years younger than her actual age. After the past year's challenges, she very easily looked and felt five years older than her fifty-three years.

Wow, Grace, she thought to herself, *looks like you need more than a few days to rest and relax. This year has definitely taken a toll on you.*

As she quietly observed herself in the mirror, her mind drifted back over the last year and all of its challenges. Tears welled up in her eyes and spilled onto her cheeks as she felt the loss of her sister again.

I wish she'd gone to the doctor when I told her to. Maybe she would have had a fighting chance. Maybe we wouldn't have had to deal with all of the insanity that is still happening with her business and family. And Kevin...

Grace shook her head as she imagined the twelve-year-old her sister left behind. His bright eyes had dimmed with sadness, not just because he had lost his mom, but he also knew the business where he liked to pretend that he was the boss that would most likely not be around much longer.

Poor little guy. He really needs me right now, but so does my business.

Grace thought about the last call she had with Joe, her best friend and Chief Operating Officer, who was amazingly supportive but stretched beyond his capacity without her. Plus, he was dealing with a separation that looked like it might end in divorce.

I truly thought he and Sandy were solid. Who would have thought they'd be here after twenty-eight years of an apparently happy marriage, children, and grandchildren! What will happen to him? And if he's distracted by life, who is running my business? My business... our business... my dad's business.

Joe had really saved her butt when her dad passed. She knew the business well, but it was going to be tough to take the lead as a woman in a time when her industry was still so male-dominated. Joe's presence had made it easier, and his operational prowess helped them scale the business quickly. He did not mind joining the company as COO because he knew that Grace was a force to be reckoned with. She took advantage of every connection she could to strategically position her woman-owned business.

I really do have a lot to be grateful for, she thought as she laid down for a much-needed nap.

Two days later, Grace was sitting in the front row at the conference with some of her industry friends. There had been some great speakers, and she was particularly excited to hear from the next one. She'd read her bio and found out that she helps business owners put plans in place in case the business owner has to leave the business either temporarily or permanently. She clapped and leaned forward in her chair while the tall, slender woman with long salt and peppered hair and a rich deep complexion walked up to the stage. Grace noticed her classically elegant style. She wore an impeccably-tailored black tweed jacket with flecks of deep yellow, cranberry, and ivory throughout. Her slacks appeared to be custom-made to fit her long legs.

Wow, she is pretty tall. Is this woman a model or a succession planner? Grace found herself preoccupied with this speaker's presence. *This lady, who has helped hundreds of business owners for more than two decades, has found a unique way to integrate her image and fashion background. What a pleasant surprise.*

As the woman walked onto the stage, I could feel her energy. It was as if a light had entered the room. Her smiling eyes spoke loudly before she even said one word. "I'm so excited to be here. As they shared in the introduction, I help business owners leave their businesses as gracefully as they've run them. I help you leave in style…"

By the end of the talk, Grace knew this was the lady who could help her get everything back on track, so she scooted out of her seat and followed Janise to the back of the room.

"Janise, thank you so much for such an amazing and easy-to-understand talk. How can I schedule some time to chat with you?"

"Thank you so much for the compliment! I am so happy that my message resonated with you. Julia, my assistant, is here with me, and she would be happy to coordinate a time to meet."

"Do you have time for lunch or dinner while we are here in Florida? I would like to chat and better understand what you do."

"I'll tell you what, let me chat briefly with these people patiently waiting behind you, and then we can meet in the lounge in about ninety minutes."

Grace smiled broadly and headed out to the chic hotel bar to find a cozy spot.

Grace sat quietly in the bar, waiting for Janise, wondering what she would say—how much she should tell this woman who might be able to help her.

As soon as the classy business woman was sitting across from her and finished ordering her drink, she initiated the conversation: "So, Grace, tell me the story of your business."

"Well, since you are speaking at our conference, I'm sure you have assumed correctly that we are in the folding carton manufacturing business. We have a team of 135 employees, and I am the CEO and majority owner. My dad started the company when my sister, Paula, and I were toddlers. Then about twenty-one years ago, dad became ill and started to really slow down. He told us that he wanted both of us to come into the business to help him out. Paula lovingly explained to Dad that she had absolutely no desire to come into the family business. Actually, she had no interest in manufacturing at all.

"Interesting. What was Paula's desire?" Janise asked.

"After college, Paula went on to serve two tours in the Air Force, discharging after working as a Special Investigations Officer. As a civilian, she briefly became a Background Investigator before asking our dad to support her dream. As a divorced mom, she knew it was going to be long hours and hard work, but she had such an extensive background in law enforcement, she wanted to take advantage of her industry expertise and transition into her own forensic private investigations firm. Paula also wanted the flexibility to be available for my little nephew, Kevin, and all his school and sports activities. When she asked Dad if he would help her start the business, he readily agreed and provided her with the financial support to get it up and running. But for me, I was destined to stay in manufacturing. I began taking over Dad's day-to-day responsibilities as his health started to decline. I love this business."

"What do you love about this business?" Janise smiled, noticing both the exhaustion and passion in Grace's voice.

"Ever since I was a child, I enjoyed coming to work with Dad. I sat quietly on his office sofa, playing with my dolls as I listened and watched him aggressively negotiate and make handshake deals. I had the freedom to walk in and out of offices and rooms. One, in particular, displayed many of our company's award-winning designs. It was such a fascinating process. All of the employees, especially the creative artists, were so kind to me and were always willing to show me what they were working on. So, I guess you can say this business appealed to both my business and creative sides." Grace paused and took a sip of her frosted Strawberry Margarita before continuing.

"When Dad passed away, I moved from being Chief Marketing Officer to Chief Executive Officer. Initially, my head was reeling. I began immediately to look at ways to innovate, increase our business presence and market share, and research the many advantages of getting certified as a woman-owned business. That decision has served us well. We were able to compete for some of the larger corporate opportunities and have grown the business to almost $30 million this year."

"That's fantastic. Do you have a partner in the business? Or did your dad leave a portion of the business to Paula?"

"No. Dad had the business valued and divided our inheritance in a way that left the business to me as a portion of my inheritance. Paula's portion included the monies Dad gave her to start *Confidential Investigation Management*. Dad was quite the planner and a great communicator. He wanted to be fair. He had seen too many of his colleague's children fighting when their parents passed away without leaving anything in writing. Some of the parents inadvertently distributed their estates in a way that favored one child over the other."

"I'm glad he was so forward-thinking because I've seen it, too. It's rough. So, then who are your partners?" Janise asked while reaching into a small leather portfolio for her notepad and pen.

"I don't have any legal partners. About six months after Dad passed, I reconnected with my dear college friend Joe Wallen when he and his wife, Sandy, learned of Dad's passing and reached out to extend their condolences. After our initial reunion, Joe and I had several lengthy conversations. We talked about the business and what I was doing to address a few challenges that could have easily gotten out of control. Joe was kind enough to share some efficient business operations advice and tips." The sunset caught her attention for a moment.

This place is so good for my soul, she thought before she continued.

"Joe, Sandy, and I got together one evening for a nice quiet dinner. During coffee and dessert, Joe hinted at some challenges he was experiencing in his current position. I wondered out loud if he would want to come work with me. After all, the three of us were inseparable in college. Even though we'd drifted apart over the years to follow our respective careers, we would always drop a quick line or email to say 'hello.' From time to time, I would read about some of the great things Joe was doing in his career. I was so proud of him. The last article I had seen was about his outstanding role in operations at some huge IT company in the San Francisco area. It was like watching a small-town kid rise to fame." Grace's face was beaming with pride as she bragged about her friend. "So, I asked Joe if he wanted to come work for me."

I'll never forget how hard he laughed when I blurted my question out loud. His weathered face scrunched with glee at the idea, and his thin biker frame shook with laughter. I felt almost embarrassed because I had just tossed this idea out with no more than a few seconds of consideration. It was a decision that would require him and his family to move and change his and Sandy's career path. I'm so glad he paused the conversation and said he and Sandy would discuss the details later and get back to me.

Grace laughed as she recalled the story. "About a week and a half later, Joe called me and said he and Sandy talked about the opportunity before them. They'd weighed the pros and cons and one thing that came out of the evening conversations was the fact that Joe did not want to work in Northern California anymore. So, he proposed the idea of coming on as my Chief Operating Officer with a pretty hefty salary package. I told him that we were doing well, but not quite *that* well. I love Joe dearly and truly value our friendship and what he brings to the table. I was candid about where we were financially and our potential. We had just become certified as a woman-owned business, and I had just embarked on a sales and marketing campaign to make the most of this new certification. I made a counter-offer that I thought was fair: As our business grew, he would receive bonuses for helping us attain certain milestones."

"Good idea!" Janise interjected.

"Thanks! Although cautiously optimistic, Joe was able to see my point of view. He knew that working with me would be far better than where he was working at that time. At least with me, he wasn't going to be stifled anymore and could stretch as a leader. He accepted my proposition, and although he is like a partner, he actually is not. Joe has been a wonderful colleague for many years. The business has grown, and our relationship is solid. But now I am concerned after seeing what happened to Paula's business and watching as Joe and Sandy's marriage shows signs of fracturing."

"What motivated you to want to talk with me about it? What can I do to help?"

Janise's smile put Grace at ease as she sensed this was going to be a warm and engaging journey.

"Well, I heard all of the good points that you addressed from the stage, and I'm terrified that I need to do something to prevent the insanity that happened in my sister's business when she died. I feel comfortable with you, and I really think you can help me find answers."

"Can you tell me a little more about Paula?" Janise gently prodded.

"Before her cancer diagnosis, Paula was the pillar of health. She was an avid skier and triathlete, and ran circles around all of us. Secretly, she was recognizing yet ignoring new ailments and alarming symptoms. Once we knew what was going on, her appearance changed in what seemed like overnight. I watched her strong, confident, and vibrant personality slowly dim, her melodic and authoritative voice become all but silent, and her tall, muscular yet feminine frame wither to less than 120 pounds. Her radiant skin became dull with a blue-gray hue. And her business…" Emotion flooded Grace's throat, and she took a deep breath to steady herself.

"Whew, sorry. I have been working around the clock for the past year, and I am simply worn out. Between that and the grief, I'm not quite myself." Grace paused again before she continued with her story. "Not only was I helping Paula at home, but I would also communicate regularly with her staff to make sure that the business was functioning as much as possible. She had grown *Confidential Investigation Management* to fifty employees, with forty of them being forensic investigators. Most of her investigators were forensic accountants and former law enforcement like herself." The memory of the sad faces of Paula's team members made her eyes well up again.

"All of those investigators were on assignment in other companies. Their job was to find theft and wrongdoing that was going on inside of the company that 'hired' them. The only people who knew that they were investigators were the owners or top executives. Paula's team respected and adored her. Some of them picked-up tasks at the office and chores around her home because they knew that I couldn't get it done by myself. After all, she was like family to them. They were all so worried about Paula and my young nephew. I would take Kevin to school while her fiancé, Dennis, would be there to pick him up. Dennis was not in a place to help out too much. He is a barber and was emotionally in shock. He had no clue of what to do when it came to the business." Grace took a deep breath and collapsed deeper into the soft leather chair.

"While all of this was going on, I also had a team of employees and customers vying for my attention. Many of our long-time employees knew Paula well and were as empathetic as can be, but they learned to stay focused and do their jobs. Joe was able to help pick up the slack, but he too became weary. When Paula passed away, we learned that, unlike Dad, she had nothing in writing. Her board of directors called a meeting to discuss what should happen next. As they reviewed her corporate documents, they realized that the bylaws and operations agreements. did very little to address how the business would continue. None of them were able to step in and stabilize the company until it could be sold. They ultimately voted to close the business." She gulped back another flood of tears at the memory of that phone call.

"That decision was devastating for everyone, including little Kevin. He sincerely thought he was going to be able to run his mom's business one day. This was so heartbreaking to watch, and it definitely got me thinking about what will happen in our business. I have bylaws and an operations agreement, but now I am not sure that is enough. I just don't want to end up with a mess like Paula's family and team faced. Still, I don't even know what to address or in what order…" Grace's weary, trembling voice trailed off to a whisper as the anxiety and uncertainty intensified.

Janise noted her anxiety and stepped right in. "It sounds like you have a few things to tackle here, but before we tackle the heavy lifting, I would like to lighten the mood for a moment. Is that okay?"

Grace took in a deep breath and exhaled, "Yes, please!"

"Okay, great, we are going to do a little reminiscing. Let's go back about twenty years in time. Do you remember when you had to step into your new role and prepare for your first big sales presentation after your dad passed?"

"Yes," Grace bubbled. "I arrived early to a major customer only to watch three of my competitors arrive, take a seat, and await their turn to present. I was the only woman in the sea of dark suits. That is when I realized I am truly in a male-dominated industry. I guess I knew before, but since I was always with Dad, it didn't seem so intimidating."

"I can only imagine what it was like back then. Being amongst all of those dark suits, did you stand out?"

Grace nearly giggled out loud at the memory of standing before the mirrored wardrobe, trying then tossing dress after dress, then suits and blazers and slacks and skirts. She wanted a look and feel that said: "You are the winner." She shook herself back to the present and proudly stated, "I did. The presentation took no time at all to develop, but the outfit—that was another story. I had no idea how to present myself as a strong professional woman."

Janise smiled broadly. "Oh yeah, I hear that from a lot of women who've been in an industry like yours. I realize that the content of the presentation is ultimately the most important component, but we must admit that confidence and the ensemble also matter."

Grace nodded in agreement.

"I asked about that part of your journey because we are going to use the ensemble as a fun way for me to unpack a potentially complex process. The wardrobe visual will serve as our road map as I introduce new information and business concepts. During our future meetings, we will create *your* perfect look. This is one of my favorite analogies to also help you better understand the work I do with women business owners."

Grace leaned forward, obviously intrigued.

"Okay, let's say that you are wanting to show up looking and feeling as strong and prepared as possible; what are the steps that you would take?"

"Well, let's see. After I have prepared the presentation, if I don't just run to the store and buy a new outfit, I would go home, walk into my closet, and think about the dresses or suits that make me feel strong."

"Like a custom-made power suit?" Janise prodded.

"Yes, exactly."

"Okay, let's go with that scenario. What does your power look consist of?"

"Well, I would work from head to toe. My face and hair would be on point, and I would choose a suit and blouse that make me feel like a winner. My jewelry would be simply stated, and I would wear my most comfortable and favorite shoes."

Janise was nodding. "So, it sounds like you would consider your audience and your desired outcome or goal. You would make sure your personal presence and style were appropriate. Your suit and blouse would fit properly, and your shoes, jewelry, and accessories would be understated?"

"Yes, that sounds about right."

"Great, let's use these areas of attention and correlate them to areas in your business. By doing this, we can illustrate in a memorable way how the seven key steps will work together to build a plan that covers some of the major aspects of your business. When we are done, your business will have that strong, powerful presence that you had on that big presentation day. Now, this might make you chuckle for a minute, but I can promise you that you won't forget it. Ready?"

Grace nodded and grabbed her pen, ready to take notes.

"Although five of the seven steps can take place in different sequences, all business owners need to do what I mentioned: Determine your 'WHY.' When preparing your mindset for our meetings, think hair and make-up. I would also like you to think about a few more things: Who are the important people in your life? Who are your most important customers? How do you solve their problems? What do you want to accomplish with your business? Then, we will take a look at your 'Personal Style' of leadership because your approach affects the day-to-day function of your business. It will also affect your business continuity."

Business continuity? I hadn't thought about how the business process would continue.

"Based on what you have shared with me, it appears that you are fast approaching the pinnacle of success which is symbolized by the 'Power Suit'—how the world sees you as empowered and in control."

Grace nodded in agreement.

"We can't forget those favorite shoes. That first impression is instantaneous and from head-to-toe. If the power suit is impeccable and the shoes aren't, you are sending a conflicting message. The shoes are for both coverage and walking. For our illustration, the shoes will represent the transitioning of your business—you walking out on your terms." Janise paused to give Grace a moment to process. "Now, let's address the purpose of the accessories. The accessories are part of the ensemble that doesn't necessarily belong solely to that suit. They are definitely a compliment and complete the look. As we look in the world of business, your accessories are comprised of a team of professional advisors engaged and tasked to impart their respective expertise. These experts are not on your payroll but are hired to address specific areas or needs. They are vital players as you begin to finalize some important decisions."

Janise sat a little taller in the leather chair as she said, "But what's an amazing look in a custom suit without great posture and composure? You will experience confidence and composure as the business increases and once you tackle the agreements and contracts that can reduce your risk. I am convinced this assignment will also increase your peace of mind when you know exactly what is in place."

Grace nodded. *That makes perfect sense!*

"Finally, the mirror represents your annual reflection and review. It is not advisable to make all of the necessary adjustments and changes to create this wonderful look if you're not going to maintain it and make sure that everything is in its proper place on a regular basis. Does this make the process more palatable?"

Grace laughed. "I have never heard such an arduous task made so simple. Let's go for it!"

Janise smiled, "Okay, so we'll start by talking about your 'WHY.' But first, let's refresh these drinks!"

Introduction

DESIGN YOUR PLAN AND CREATE PEACE OF MIND

CHANCES ARE YOU have experienced a moment like this, receiving a call from a longtime friend and business associate informing you that one of your favorite colleagues has been in a critical accident or died either suddenly or after a long-term illness.

Like Grace, you may be facing that burst of emotion that comes when you think of your own mortality and wonder, *If this could happen to my friends, what could happen to me? What would happen to my business if I were to become too sick to go to work or run my business? How would my team and customers fare if I were on extended disability? How would this affect the stability of the strong business foundation we have created?* You're used to putting out fires and putting other people's priorities ahead of your own. However, while taking care of everyone else, you may have lost sight of the concept that taking care of yourself is a part of taking care of everyone else. You're probably feeling a bit overwhelmed at the mere idea of a significant hiccup in the business and the ripple effect that could derail your industry standing and financial stability. Maybe your stomach begins to churn at the thought of rollercoasters and downward spirals.

So, what do you do? You have the greatest intentions of putting a plan in place someday. And for some reason, someday never finds its way onto your calendar. By the time you settle in, you notice one thing: Time has passed and there is still no plan for the future. In sheer panic and desperation, you pick up a book that might help. Good news, this one will.

You're Not Alone

CEOs face crises every single day. You start your day with calls and emails reminding you that your purpose is to build and serve an empire. Maybe you actively advocate and navigate the regulations and laws that affect your industry and its future growth. Perhaps your unspoken goal is also to become a top employer in your region. As a result, you put a lot of emphasis on taking care of your employees because they do a great job of taking care of your customers. But what would happen if a significant crisis took you out of your business for an extended length of time?

When these severe crises happen with no preparation, they turn into an avalanche of challenges that feel never-ending. One's employees, customers, and entire livelihood and future hang in the balance. Without a succession plan, everyone will eventually lose. With one, everyone can navigate a turbulent time with more ease and intention.

A plan is the first step to gaining control and turning your circumstances around. Creating a leadership emergency preparedness plan gives your entire team a road map and vision as to how to move forward if something horrible happens to you. It could literally save your life and business.

How do I know? Well…

Let Me Introduce Myself

First, I am a business owner who has worked with business owners over the past twenty years. My career and this journey have taken me through various aspects of the financial services world. My initial focus was on retirement planning because that is what I learned working at two of the nation's largest insurance companies. After educating employees on the advantages and benefits of participating in their 401k plan, I couldn't help but be distracted by the thoughts that the business owners did not have a plan for the business's future. It did not matter how great the 401k plan was because there would be no business left to continue the retirement plan. There would be no customers or employees. It made no sense to put a great plan in place for employees that would no longer have a job. That really bothered me. However, working alongside driven CEOs, I often wondered what it would take to get the business owners to slow down long enough to plan for themselves and the legacy of their business?

And then it happened to a colleague of mine. I witnessed the immediate dismantling of a business when the owner was killed in an accident. The employees had nowhere to go, and the customers were scrambling to replace that service provider. My natural curiosity kicked in, and I began to question why such a successful professional would not have a plan in place. My heart broke when I learned that his board of directors got together, and since (like Paula's board) there was nothing in writing, a vote was taken to close the business.

A few years later, while serving as local president for the National Association of Insurance and Financial Advisors, one of my duties was speaking to the media and sharing information during Life Insurance Awareness Month (September), specifically on the importance of creating a family business plan. During one particular meeting with the local newspaper's business editor, he asked, "What is it that you do?" I explained, "I help business owners put a plan in place just in case they don't make it back to work either temporarily or permanently. One of the tools that we share is the benefits of life insurance." His following comment took me by surprise and also enlightened me: "I didn't know that you can use life insurance in a business." That's when I got my answer. If the business editor, who reviews and publishes business content and information daily, doesn't know that you can use life insurance in business, how many business owners did not know the same? What other tools do they not know about?

Within the financial services industry, business succession planning is viewed as "advanced planning." There is a lot of detail and time spent understanding the nuances of business planning. If those of us in the industry need to be educated and become familiar with the terms, how can we expect business owners to know these topics and how to address them? I quickly realized that most business owners did not have any idea of how to begin to create a financial plan to sustain their business after a long-term disability and death. What if I were able to create awareness? What if I could help business owners learn to articulate what they wanted?

I noticed that many of the business owners who did have plans could have a team of experts surrounding them and bringing great advice and recommendations. Unfortunately, not all business owners are in a place to have Mergers and Acquisitions experts or a team of lawyers and advisors. They may be a business owner who has a need but no idea where to begin.

Every Business Owner Needs a Plan

I decided to write this book because I wanted to help business owners like you navigate the journey towards a successful succession regardless of your business size. After all, mortality is the great equalizer. I also wanted to take a complex conversation and make it easier to approach and understand. My desire is to help you solve a problem that may be keeping you up at night, either consciously or unconsciously.

I decided to write it with a story, quick lessons, and exercises to add a little bit of levity and fun to a challenging topic. Studies have shown that we learn and retain more when we have fun and listen to great stories. You will have a simplified tour as to where to start and how to finish the process.

You're going to follow Grace, a character who will represent almost every CEO I've ever met. Grace's journey may be similar to yours, or maybe it's the journey of someone you know. You will likely have more in common with Grace than differences.

Disclaimers

This content and my approach will likely make you smile and sometimes feel a little shifty in your seat. Both emotions are normal and beneficial. After all, planning is done by those who care for and about others.

The story and information are being shared to help you better prepare for your future and the future of your business. This is not a personal consultation, nor is it personal advice. I am not an attorney, nor am I providing legal advice. I am not an accountant and not providing tax advice or investment advice. Before making any changes in your business, it is essential that you consult with your attorney, accountant, financial advisors, and anyone else required to make the changes that are to be made in your business. If you do not have advisors, read on to learn how to bring the right team together and better engage them.

Rest assured, Grace is not an actual client. This kind of work in planning is definitely a confidential process. Grace is more like an archetype of the clients in my practice and those I have encountered. I have witnessed so many losses and battles over the past two-plus decades. There is no confidential information being disclosed without the express permission of any client. This story may have similarities to yours; however, this is a fictional character, and the similarities are purely coincidental or the result of you recognizing an archetype that is one you embody to some degree.

How to Read the Book

Please read it from start to finish because it's delivered in a very intentional order. I realize it is tempting to look at all of the things you have on your plate and just thumb through, searching for chapter highlights or the "Cliff Notes" version. Resist the urge to go to the chapter with the title you think you need and do a quick scan. (Yes, I told you—I'm a business owner too, and I know all the ways we take shortcuts because we can.) However, this is not one of those projects where shortcuts are beneficial in the long run. Creating a wholistic plan is heart-centered work that is best applied when taking small steps to reach the desired goal with the greatest ease.

Hopefully, this book will stimulate lots of thoughts, ideas, and questions. This is a safe space, time, and place to ask all of those questions. Grab a journal to write down your thoughts, ideas, and feelings. It will be beneficial in the future to look back on the details of this journey while moving forward with your own plans, conversations, and research. This may be done pen to paper or electronically. You know your learning style best, so use the technique that works best for you.

Make notes pertinent to your own story and the next steps. As ideas and potential scenarios come to mind, be sure to jot them down. There may be a more profound understanding needed in that area and a visual scenario may be especially helpful for you to articulate the questions you may have.

Do the work in small steps. When researching certain aspects of planning, take it one step at a time. This type of planning could appear to be deceptively simple. In fact, the process will reveal the depth and introspection needed to navigate the deeper end of the pool. Addressing your strategy in order will help keep you on track and not lose sight of the greater outcome.

Finally, find someone to help you, as external reflection is much-needed once you get into this process. It may be a great idea to have a reading partner who is also a business professional so that the two of you can discuss some of the concepts learned. It may also be important to hire other business professionals, coaches, or consultants. Consider them all. They all come with a level of expertise that may be beneficial to your growth and your process. To learn more about the subject, you could go to "Extended Conversations with Grace" at www.LeavingInStyle.com/Resources.

I'm ready. Are you?

Are you ready to design a plan and create peace of mind? Are you prepared to embrace this journey and get started in making your ideal plan? Grab your favorite beverage, along with Grace, and let's get started! Let's go!

Chapter One
CLARIFY YOUR WHY

AS SOON AS Grace and Janise refreshed their drinks and settled back into the soft leather chairs in the bar, Janise got started. "From the story you told me, I can see there are a lot of things that are very important to you, Grace, and the first thing I like to do is start with learning more about *why* they are important to you. In an effort to get a clearer understanding of the big picture, I would like to ask a few questions to get started. Ready?"

Grace nervously shuffled in her seat, slowly nodded to the affirmative, and then took another sip of her Margarita.

"I am getting the feeling that this is an urgent matter for you. Can you tell me why this is so important right now?" Janise prompted.

Grace's intertwined fingers grasped the stem of her glass as she thought about her answer. "Well, I have seen what's going on in Paula's business, and I don't want to see that happen in my business. I have loyal employees and loyal customers, and the business is growing. I have a loyal business executive and two amazing children who rely on me. So, I certainly don't want to see any legal issues come up or any fighting or misunderstandings that I could have prevented. I would hate to see my competition just walk in and take over my business because there's nothing in writing, or simply close the doors—well, I don't want either to be a possibility. I couldn't imagine my employees being out on the street with no job. It would be a nightmare to call a meeting, stand in front of my employees, and tell them we were closing our doors because we didn't have a plan for life's events."

"Yes, I imagine that would be a nightmare. The good news is that it's avoidable. Do you have any idea what your business value is, Grace?"

"Not at the moment. We had a preliminary evaluation done twenty years ago. Still, we haven't had any conversations on what our business's true value is today. I would also hate to be in a position where, God forbid, something happens to Joe; and Sandy would be relying on me to help her when Joe's salary is gone. As much as I love Sandy, she is not the best at saving money—she is a teacher and has relied on Joe to handle all things financial since they have been married. I would like to have a continued friendship with Sandy, but I definitely do not want to become her caretaker. Plus, Joe and Sandy are discussing divorce after all these years. Of course, I am concerned about them personally, and I'm not sure if I should be concerned professionally. After all, he is a key employee who has a lot to lose. Personal matters can become quite the distraction." Grace gulped her last statement down with another sip of her drink.

"Yes, we would definitely need to take this into consideration," Janise answered. "So, what would happen to your children if there was not a plan in place?"

"I really don't know!" Grace's voice was tight with fear. "My children have not participated in the business, although my son has expressed some interest. I don't know what would happen to them or anything, quite frankly, and it scares me."

"This is a terrifying spot to be in. The good news is that you're not oblivious to it, as some business owners are. Do you have a will and a trust?"

"Well, I'm not sure because I always get those two confused. Can you be a little bit clearer as to what those are?" Grace put her drink down and grabbed her notepad and pen again.

"Sure! A will is a legal document that governs your wishes regarding how you want your minor children cared for and how you want your personal property distributed. If you want to leave certain things such as family heirlooms to certain people, you can have that written into your will. A trust is a third-party agreement that holds assets on behalf of your beneficiaries. It is often used to minimalize estate taxes. Without a trust, your beneficiaries may have to go to court and work through the probate process. When going through probate, all of your assets and information in the court document become public information. Suppose you have property that you want to be distributed outside of the roving public eye. In that case, you will want to talk with an estate planning attorney."

"Okay, I do not have a trust. And I have a will, but it is just something that I wrote out years ago when I was going on a trip." Grace's face was scrunched with concern.

"Don't worry. These are some of the deeper conversations we will talk about later and will also require professional legal advice and support. Can you tell me what you have in place now as far as business continuity?"

"Yes. Joe and I, of course, can take over one of each other's roles, if it's temporarily for a short length of time. When it comes to our team and our staff, we have certain managers that are crossed-trained and can step in and help in different areas if that's what you mean."

"Yes, I often think of business and leadership planning as emergency preparedness. We don't have to wait for a natural disaster to come along or for something catastrophic to happen that would shake up how the flow of business works.

"I agree," replied Grace.

"Great, so we could also look at what kind of strategy you have in place for your leadership and the growth of your leadership?"

"Absolutely! That would be wonderful."

"As essential leaders, do you and Joe have a plan for income replacement if one of you were out?"

"Do you mean disability?" Grace asked for some clarity.

"Yes, that's exactly right."

"Well, kind of. We do have a small disability policy that is similar to what our employees have."

"Okay, well, in the event of disability, will that small policy cover your household expenses?"

"No. I'm sure it won't. We just got it because we didn't know what we needed, but we knew it was better than having nothing at all." Again, Grace's eyebrows were furrowed with concern.

"Don't worry, Grace. You're in the right place at the right time. Now, can you tell me a little bit about what you and he have as a plan for retirement?"

"Yes, we both participate in our company's 401k plan. We must be extremely careful and make sure that our contributions do not exceed what our employees are contributing. We made that mistake before and were penalized as a result. That was no fun! Plus, we both have investments outside of the business."

"So, you're looking for ways to get greater tax advantages?" Janise asked.

"Absolutely!" I exclaimed.

"Have you and Joe talked about what retirement potentially looks like? Have you set a date or looked at how you would leave the business?" Janise continued her line of questioning.

"You know, we talk lightly about it, but we end up saying that this business is our retirement plan."

"I hear that so often, Grace, but what does it mean to you?" Janise sipped her sparkling water.

"Well, I don't know. It's just something that we always say. The reality is that if our business is indeed our retirement plan, we would have to find a way to either sell the business and make a good profit. Or, as we get older, we would have to find someone to come and run the day-to-day part of the business. In that case, we would continue to own the business and benefit from its growth."

"Do you want to sell the business?" One of Janise's eyebrows was raised with curiosity.

"No, not really. Again, we haven't talked about it. Since my dad started the business, I would like my son to be in a position to continue with the business if that's what he chooses to do. Both Joe and I definitely want to have options. We want to be able to work in the business if we choose to or to travel and give back to our charities and churches if we choose to, as well." The furrowed brow relaxed as Grace talked about the charities she was supporting.

"Do you feel that the business still has room to grow?" Janise probed.

"Oh yes! With technology, we are finding new and better ways to increase productivity and meet the demands of some of our best customers."

"As you look at growing the business, are you looking at using your own capital, or are you looking to grow by using loans or engaging investors?"

"Well, Joe and I've talked about growing the business. We've also talked about growing it over time and in a scalable way because we've seen other businesses implode with growth that was too fast! We don't want to bring in other investors either. All that said, we would have to think about taking out a business loan in the future, but we haven't sat down to look at what those numbers are going to be and how we truly want to do it."

"It sounds like a lot is going on; it's a lot of moving parts." Janise reflected back on Grace's reality but without all the overwhelm.

"Yes, there are! And that's why I think it's best to talk to you right now because if we get a lot of these balls in the air and something happens to either one of us, we could end up like Paula. Here today and gone tomorrow." Grace's eyes teared up a little as she thought about how quickly she'd lost her sister and how fast her sister's business had failed.

"You mentioned you have two children, Grace. Do you have a life partner?"

"No, my ex and I divorced when the children were small. I have been so busy in this business that I haven't really taken a lot of time for myself. So, not only do I not have a partner, but I'm also not dating at this time either—especially after this last year!"

"Yeah, it is hard to do it all, isn't it? Now, earlier, you mentioned getting your business certified as a woman-owned business. Can you tell me what your vision is for leveraging that certification?"

"Yes, I'm especially proud of that status and want to grow in that space. I know there are a lot of corporate and subcontracting opportunities that I could leverage. Still, I haven't looked into them just yet."

"Yes, we'll definitely have to make that conversation a priority. Now, can you tell me about the relationship that you have with your employees?" Janise continued down her list of questions.

"We have absolutely wonderful employees! Many of them have been with us since Dad was in the business. In fact, we were nominated and won, as one of the Top Employers in our industry! We are so proud of our accomplishments and the employees that we have trained in our business. I hear some of the other owners complain about their employees and what a waste of time they are or how lazy they are. I can't help but wonder why they don't invest in quality people. That's what we did. We took the time to invest in our employees by training them, and we get referrals for new employees from our excellent employees. It has worked extremely well for us. In fact, in some parts of our business, we have a couple of generations of family members who have come to work for us because they know us to be a fair employer."

Janise smiled and set down her notepad and pen. "Well, Grace. First, I want to congratulate you on growing such a great business. I know the time and effort and tears and fears that go into making sure that every aspect of a business grows and operates smoothly. It sounds like you and Joe have done an outstanding job. I can see that your *WHY* for this conversation around success(ion) planning is truly motivated by a genuine desire. You want to make sure that your business is built to last for your children. It is important to know that every employee you have would be taken care of if something were to happen to your leadership team."

Grace nodded while Janise took a sip of her water, then settled back into the chair and began addressing the fears that had sparked this conversation. "In the case of Paula's business, it sounds like she waited a little too long to put a plan in place. It is often a lot easier to strategize when there's no emergency; it also costs a lot less. Since Paula was sick, her options were limited to what was available under those conditions. The cost was her business. It's unfortunate, and I'm sorry you had to witness it and bear so much of the burden." Janise's compassionate gaze made Grace feel like the woman before her had seen many situations like this in her past and knew the pain from firsthand experience.

"One of the nice things about having this conversation while you are still young, Grace, is that it gives you time to actually put together a strategy and plan. Many business owners aren't aware that it may take at least eighteen months and even up to five years or more to have a nice and smooth transition. Did you know it took Michael Eisner with Disney ten years to name a suitable successor?"

"Wow, I didn't realize it took that long! I guess that gives us something to think about."

"Unfortunately, the successor didn't stay very long, but you get the point. Life happens, and it just takes a lot of planning and focus and making sure that you have the right team. Time allows you to select the right people to be in the right seats. Attempting to put a viable plan in place while under duress is what I refer to as "crisis planning." This type of planning can be devastating to the company and the successors because you may not get the best candidate and leaders in place when rushing a process. Crisis planning could also be a very expensive journey, as it also puts you at the mercy of the vendor supplying the products or services at the eleventh hour.

You know who your competition is, and they know who you are. Suppose they sense there is trouble in paradise. In that case, they will pay attention closely and watch as your market share declines. Your service may deteriorate, and customers may begin to flee. Your key employees could begin to leave to seek stability, and ultimately your business could fail. Once the downward spiral gains momentum, they could swoop in and buy it at a bargain and, in some cases, get it for free. So much for that retirement plan!"

Grace shook her head in understanding. *I can't let this happen to our business!*

"Can you imagine what happened to those business owners who didn't plan in time and woke up one day and decided they wanted to retire just as the economy started to decline?"

"Unfortunately, I saw that happen during the Great Recession of 2008. It was devastating! Several of our colleagues could not sell their businesses because there were no buyers. They also had to continue to work as the business was disappearing right before their eyes. Of course, with that business's failure, so went all of their retirement dreams. Some of them lost everything, including their homes. I know of one couple who had to move in with their adult son and his family. Others were looking forward to a life of retirement, travel, leisure, and tranquility. Instead, they are now in a room next to a three-year-old and a five-year-old. As much as they love their grandchildren, it is not exactly tranquil."

"That is exactly what we can work to avoid. Another factor that is not often considered is the regulatory changes that could affect how your business model works. If you at least have a base strategy, you can pivot and readjust a lot easier than having no strategy at all. As you can see, it clearly doesn't pay to procrastinate."

"Yes, I can definitely see that," Grace said, still feeling a little wide-eyed and overwhelmed.

"I'm so glad we were able to chat today. There are a lot of ways to approach some of your major concerns. I would love to support you through the process of putting yourself in the most powerful position possible. Would you like to discuss what it would be like for us to work together?"

Grace nodded as relief flooded her entire body. "Yes, I've found this conversation very helpful already, and I appreciate how you make everything so clear and palatable. This is something I want to get started on right away and I certainly need your help. What is the next step?"

"Now that I have a better understanding of what you want to accomplish, let's plan to gather, prioritize, and organize your key performance indicators. We will create a six-month timeline to get the core competencies in place. Based on our conversation, and your desire for one-on-one coaching, our Haute Couture program would best meet your needs."

"Haute Couture?" Grace questioned. "That sounds fancy."

"I guess you can say it's *our* version of fancy." Janise smiled. "My team and I realize that business owners have different needs and levels of desired engagement, and we wanted to keep the theme of Style when identifying our Leaving In Style offerings. In the world of fashion, Haute Couture represents the highest level of fashion. It is a French term which means 'highly handmade.' These are the finest of garments, and are custom-fitted just for you."

"Well, right now, I could use that kind of 'made-for-you' personal touch," Grace agreed. "I am curious. What are your other programs?"

"Well, I also coach business owners who want to achieve results in a shorter time frame, either because they have done some of the preliminary work or they have an urgent deadline to meet. Our three-month option for coaching is the Couture program. The term Couture is French for dressmaking and is more often used as a reference to high fashion or designer clothing. A business owner can start with three months of coaching and continue into the six-month option if it makes sense."

"I know we are talking about my manufacturing business, but I am getting a New York Fashion Week vibe."

Janise laughed. "Yes! Instead of using the age-old and sometimes confusing sports analogies, I thought it would be more enjoyable to use the flare of fashion and style."

"That makes a lot of sense." Grace exclaimed. "Not all of us understand the basketball, golf, and football analogies that are always thrown around in business books and meetings. This is a refreshing break."

"Thank you. I am glad that you like them. Many years ago, I was an athlete and I do understand most of the terminology, but I can recall so many women getting annoyed and frustrated by all of the sports metaphors because they did not understand those points of reference."

"This is certainly a welcome relief. Are there any more fashionable business offerings?" Grace asked.

"Yes, there are. Our entry into business and succession coaching is a Bespoke online course."

"Bespoke? I have never heard that term."

"It is a British term that defines an item, usually clothing, that is tailor-made. This seven-week online course is tailor-made for business owners. It is ideal for those who prefer a self-study approach to learning and taking action. We are so excited about this course because it allows for us to help business owners any time of day, anywhere in the world."

"I can hear the excitement in your voice when you talk about a solution for business owners around the world," Grace interjected.

"Oh yes! You may recall from my on-stage introduction, I have coached business owners in various aspects of their journey from starting businesses to scaling, to preparing for exit for more than two decades. This is sometimes hard work, but it is also 'heart work.' Of course, it's important to share here that I also work with other professionals that you will learn more about who are uniquely qualified to review, analyze, and address a business owner's financial and protection needs as warranted."

"Thank you for the overview, Janise. It gives me a better idea of how my business can be helped and where I fit in. Your assessment is correct, the Haute Couture timeline works best for me. This all sounds so exciting! I am actually looking forward to this journey!"

"It is so good to see that you are ready to get started, Grace. Let's take a look at our calendars and schedule our first meeting. You never know how soon you're going to need to have this in place. How does next Friday look to you?"

"Next Friday. Yes, how about 9 am?" Grace asked.

"Perfect, let me get your card." Janise said as she passed hers to Grace.

No time to lose

"I will email you in the next couple of days to gather some additional business information. After I have reviewed everything, I will go over in detail how our process works as we move forward. We will discuss benchmarks and a projected timeline for getting things done, and we will plan to meet monthly for the next six months. I look forward to tracking your success and then reviewing the 'key performance indicators' this time next year. Once we finalize the details, I will send you an email link to the terms of our agreement for review, approval, and signature." Janise smiled, picked up her purse, and held it on her lap. "Grace, it has been an absolute pleasure. I have a feeling that you will make the most of our time together. I can't wait to start working with you."

"Thank you, Janise! I'm so grateful. See you soon," Grace held back her tears of relief as she shook Janise's hand and then headed back to her room for a little rest and relaxation.

Prepare to Leave In Style at:
www.LeavingInStyle.com/Resources

Chapter Two

IDENTIFY YOUR PERSONAL
STYLE OF BUSINESS LEADERSHIP

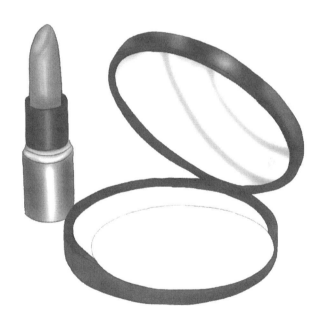

GRACE EXCUSED HERSELF from a breakroom chat with a few of her employees and hurried to her office for her first meeting with Janise. Fortunately, she'd already downloaded the software required to meet via video conference and had everything cued up to join the meeting. Even with all of that, she logged in two minutes late.

Janise's smiling face appeared on her screen. "Good morning, Grace. How are you today?"

"Good morning. I'm well. Sorry I'm a couple of minutes late. I got caught up with a few of my employees in the break room."

"It's no problem at all," Janise smiled genuinely. "I've been looking forward to our meeting. But before we dive in, I can't help but notice the incredible display behind you. I'm assuming those are some of your packages? And pictures of your... team?" Janise was squinting into the camera, eyes obviously focused on the bookshelves behind Grace.

"Oh yes." Grace turned over her right shoulder and pointed at the display. "Those are our award-winning boxes—some of my absolute favorites!" She smiled back at Janise and then glanced over her left shoulder. "The pictures next to the business certifications and leadership awards are pictures of my team here, and these are family pictures." She brought each picture a little closer to the camera so Janise could see. "This is my father and me, standing in front of our first building. And this is Joe and me, standing in that same place the day he agreed to be my 'partner in crime.' This is my son, here at the office, helping us with his first job assignment of loading corrugated cases onto pallets. And this is my sister and me." She paused as she felt the heaviness in her chest expand for a moment.

I miss her.

"Thank you so much for indulging me. As you probably noted when we first spoke, I love fashion and design in spaces, too." Janise sat back in her chair again and continued, "I especially love how you have given such care to acknowledging your success and the people who are most important to you."

"Well, I couldn't do any of this without them." Grace smiled back at her, noticing how much care Janise had put into her space and how she showed up, even over a video conference. Her silky teal wrap blouse was accessorized with diamond stud earrings and a simple silver necklace with a pendant. Her hair and makeup were natural and stunning. The classic simplicity of her style was reflected in the light décor behind her as well. A simple painting of sunflowers hung behind her on the blue-grey wall.

I feel a bit underdressed in my coral blouse, khakis, and turquoise stone necklace, but that's how I roll here at the office.

"Yes, it's so important to have great employees, and it sounds like you've been careful to recruit and retain people who actually care about your business and the work they do. Many years ago, I read Jim Collins' *Good To Great*. One of the ideas that resonated with me and continues to do so to this day is the concept of having the right bus, with the right people on the bus and, in the right seats on that bus. And that's where I'd like to focus our conversation today."

"Great! I love talking about my team," Grace replied as she leaned back in her comfortable yet worn leather chair and settled in for the conversation, notebook, and pen ready on the whitewashed wooden desk in front of her.

"Let's start with the basics. Do you have a succession plan or business continuation plan in any form in place right now?" Janise picked up her pen and waited for her reply.

"We have a basic idea of what we would like to see happen in the event of an emergency. However, a lot of what we have planned are just ideas, and we don't have a lot of them in writing."

It's time to get these details written down. I'm so glad she's here to help me finally get this done.

"Have you and Joe had any conversations about your vision for the future of this business and how it would continue without one or both of you?" Janise questioned.

"I can't say that we have. Joe and I have never discussed the long-term vision of how this business would run and grow or how we would ultimately get out of the company. We really just hit the ground running on operations and have been focused on business growth and employee and customer satisfaction. I wouldn't be surprised if we have different ideas of what that means and how it will affect us."

"It's not unusual for leaders and partners to get caught up in the day-to-day and not find time to look to the future. So, let's take a moment, Grace, and walk into the future together. What does it look like to you after you leave this business?"

"I see myself enjoying sunny days on the beaches of Southern California and giving back to my community. I have a strong passion for assisting young women business owners as they create a path towards success. There is so much that I have learned in this wonderful life, and I am sure I have plenty to contribute so that others don't have to make some of the mistakes that I have made."

I've made some doozies! Grace shook her head at some of the memories that immediately surfaced.

"Do you see the same for Joe?" Janise continued.

"Oh no, my old pal Joe and I get along wonderfully, but we are quite different. I think Joe would probably move to the Midwest and live on a huge farm. He also enjoys fly-fishing and has dreams of sitting on a porch watching the sway of the trees and relishing in the quiet serenity that comes with being outside of the big city."

Janise nodded affirmatively. "Both options sound quite peaceful and very different. This is what needs to be taken into consideration when looking at how and when you will both leave the business."

"Yes, I've been thinking since our first meeting that Joe and I should sit down and work through that process. We love our employees and would want them to feel safe and secure and work here as long as they'd like, whether we are here or not. That sounds like a homework assignment?"

"Yes, it is. There are a few things that I would like for you to consider during that meeting…"

Grace grabbed her pen and pulled her notebook a little closer.

"Take a look at your entire business. Look at all aspects of the business and break it down by department. Identify the needs and attributes of each department, paying particular attention to the leadership and employees. Do you have roles and responsibilities for each position? Do you know the value that they bring to the company? Do you have a human resources manager?"

"I'll address the easy one first. Yes, we have one full-time employee and one part-time employee working in human resources. Whenever we have a need beyond what these ladies can do, we work with an outsourced human resource professional. We have some of our newer positions clearly identified. Still, I must be honest—we have not gone back to fully spell out what some of our long-standing position employees are doing or should be doing. We know the value of each position, but we have not consciously thought about the value each employee offers."

"Do you think that your human resources team can help you develop the employees in the roles that they are in? Would they be able to add insight as to the employees who need to change roles?"

"Yes, we have a fantastic team, and they have been eager to bring in education and continuous development opportunities to the company. I think they would be on board with this assignment."

"That sounds great. Let's start with understanding who all the players are and then looking at how we can build them up to help them grow the company. We will put timelines and strategies to this later."

"I love this stuff! We have excellent employees, and I am sure they would be more than willing to learn and cross-train to support one another." Grace's heart warmed as the faces of her employees drifted across her mind.

I really do have the best employees.

"Great. Now, I've discovered that a SWOT analysis is a good tool for analyzing the potential growth in an employee, as well as the business itself."

"A SWOT analysis. Hmmm… I had not thought about that as a measuring tool. Will you please refresh my memory on what we're looking at?" Grace wrote SWOT on the page and waited for her explanation.

"Of course. S is for strength. This is an opportunity to look at what attributes the employee brings to the company and their position. The W is for weaknesses, as it is important to look at where an employee has room for improvement and growth. The growth that they bring to their position may be what is needed to stabilize a deficiency." She paused to give me time to capture the ideas on the page. "The O is for opportunities."

Grace jumped in before she continued. "I have a long list of ideas in this area. Some come from our online feedback portal."

"That is a great place to get them. When you can see and share constructive feedback that has come directly from interactions, it becomes a real-world learning tool."

Grace nodded in agreement. "Yes, we share them with our team at our weekly meetings. Making that direct connection and some modifications has done wonders for our satisfaction ratings. Those satisfied responses have led to more business, new contracts, and even introductions to other potential customers."

Janise grinned and continued. "And the T is for threats."

"Threats?"

"Yes, threats."

"Tell me more," Grace invited.

"Threats can come from almost anywhere. Right now, we want a focus on those affecting the employees. Are your employees following safety protocol? Are they careless with Internet access, passwords, and practices? Are they a weak link when it comes to productivity? How does that weak link affect the company overall? By addressing each department's threats, you will recognize holes that could be expensive or devastating liabilities. Acknowledging these threats can help you better educate and train your employees. This is a good place to get support from your human resources team. There is so much more that can go into employee assessments and engagement, but this will give you a good start. By looking at the entire team and analyzing the SWOT analysis as a whole, training and development strategies can be created to reduce the threats and address the growth opportunities."

Grace put her pen down and looked up into Janise's face again. "I can see how this type of analysis will not only help us plan for the future, but we can potentially see the benefits of growing sooner than later. In essence, this is not one of those long-term goal plans that we have to plant seeds and wait patiently as they grow. With action steps, we will see the fruits of our labor. This can almost become instant gratification."

Janise was nodding again. "Another benefit to the analysis is that you can come to some tough but substantiated conclusions. Are your employees on the right bus? If so, are they in the right seat on the right bus? Hopefully, over time, the answer will be 'yes' for those who belong. With your blessings, those who do not belong can be encouraged to find their calling in a career or company that will make them happy."

"I agree. We do have a few employees who I believe will recognize that this is not the place for them. By sitting down with them and addressing the areas in which we need to see substantial improvements, they may see that as an opportune time to acknowledge that they do not want to do what it takes to excel in their position and decide to leave with no hard feelings. It would be great if they could see where their strengths lie and seek employment in a place that complements their attributes and then soar in that position with their new employer."

"So, you are on board with making that happen?" Janise's eyebrows went up with excitement.

"I sure am." Grace nodded and sat back in her chair again.

"Awesome. Now that we have taken care of the employees, it is time for you to do the same for the company. When creating a SWOT analysis for the company, one task is to create an overall plan that includes an assessment that provides a step-by-step roadmap for how the company will develop, design, implement, and evaluate its progress."

"Since we have just looked at our operations, sales, marketing, logistics, and service departments, what is there left to consider?"

"Good question. We can continue to fine-tune the employees and each department, but now it is time to look at the big picture of what I like to call the big WHY. Why do you do what you do? What is the company's mission? Do the employees know this mission? Do they see the big picture? Do they approach their work with that mission in mind? What is the vision for the company? Is that a conversation had outside of the executive offices? A unified message can become the beacon desperately needed to light the way. The well-lit path, with the right employees on it, can minimize uncertainty, unite the team, and foster loyalty." Janise paused to give Grace a chance to respond.

"I can see how our business can be elevated immediately by taking the time to pay more attention to the infrastructure, even before attempting to address a departure."

"Exactly. Frequently, both the present and future can be addressed simultaneously. There simply needs to be a clear strategy and instructions. Some tasks must be delegated to key employees. Deadlines must be set and met, and the next step would be to reconvene and triage the findings."

Grace nodded to let her know that she was following.

"There is one more essential strategy that must be considered. This could be the most critical area that can add fuel to the engine. You and Joe must address the leadership and management styles that affect your team. When we were in Florida, you may recall me likening this process to getting dressed for that big sales presentation. Well, let's consider your leadership style to equate to your overall personal style. Just as in your personal style, your leadership style says a lot about who you are, your attention to detail, and what is important to you. Both your personal and leadership style silently orchestrate and dictate how others may initially see you. Once the impression is set, they will watch to see what you do next. If you are meticulous, poised, and self-assured, we can liken that to your leadership style being confident, inclusive, and forward-thinking. "The two of you need to take a look at your respective leadership styles and those of your key employees and potential successors. Do you have a team of critical thinkers? Are you visionaries or micro-managers? Is your team, on any level, relying on you to make decisions for them, or are they empowered to make decisions? When looking at the leadership styles and aligning them with your goals, both must work in concert to stabilize or scale the business."

"You know, I had not thought about that. There are times we and our styles do become quite confusing to our employees. Some of our best employees get frustrated because Joe does not allow them to make some of the most straightforward decisions. In fact, we have had some superstar salespeople leave because they felt they had no direction, no voice, and way too much micro-managing. I had not thought about how our leadership styles could be affecting our stability and our bottom line." Grace jotted down "Leadership Styles" and looked back up at the screen.

"It's something worth thinking about. Suppose either of you were gone temporarily or permanently. Would your employees feel empowered enough to jump in and run this business? At this point, we have determined that you have the right team of employees; now, it's time to empower them to do what they do best."

"This is great, Janise. I'm thrilled about this idea of looking at our unique styles and making sure our employees could jump in at any time. Joe and I will certainly spend time looking at how we, too, can grow in this area."

"I look forward to hearing how these conversations unfold with you two. How long do you think you will need to accomplish that list?"

Grace paused and reviewed her notes. "I think we could probably have the conversations and some good information for you in about ten to twelve days."

"Fantastic. Let's set next month's meeting now," Janise said as she pulled out her calendar.

Once they had plotted their next appointment together, Grace grinned wryly at her. "Janise, thank you so much for today. I haven't been this excited about homework in a long time."

"My pleasure! See you soon." She waved quickly before ending the meeting.

Wow, this is going to be amazing. I can't wait to dive in.

Prepare to Leave In Style at:
www.LeavingInStyle.com/Resources

Chapter Three

TAILOR YOUR SYSTEMS FOR GROWTH

"GRACE, HELLO. HOW are you?" Janise asked as soon as her face came into view.

"I'm excellent, actually. That conversation with Joe went exceptionally well. We discovered some crucial information through our business- and employee- SWOT analyses. Our findings are going to help us fill in some gaps on our team and prepare them for a future without us."

"I love hearing that. Tell me about the conversation with Joe…" she prompted.

Grace sat back in her chair and started to tell Janise about her week. "As Joe and I started talking about the idea of not being here one day, his initial reaction was to repeat, 'But we are fine.' After hearing him say that for the fourth time, I put down my pen, looked him in the eyes, and reminded him that we are not invincible. Yes, we are fine today, but we have no guarantees. Of course, Joe knows this to be true because he was here as Paula became ill. He finally acknowledged that he did not want to think of his own mortality and had hoped those dismissive answers would allow him to be able to gloss over the tough stuff."

"Good for him for seeing and acknowledging that!" Janise exclaimed.

"Yes! And then we were able to make progress. We held the first round of meetings with our human resources team. We then set up meetings with all of our employees, starting with the managers and then moving down the organization chart, eventually getting to our new and part-time employees. We had everyone complete a SWOT analysis on the department they work in, the position they hold, and themselves. In addition to learning a lot about how well we are doing as a company, we addressed new action items to tackle and our immediate improvement areas. We also learned that most of our employees are loyal and want the best for the company." Grace smiled, happy with her achievements.

"Well, that is fantastic. Based on what you have shared, we are off to a good start in identifying and measuring some of the key performance indicators. If you don't mind, send me the tasks and goals you have uncovered, and I will include them in our master plan."

"Yes, that would be great. Thank you!" Grace could already feel the heaviness of an uncertain future falling away.

This lady is a godsend!

"And how about the company's financial analysis?" Janise asked.

"Oh, well... pulling together spreadsheets, analyzing our cost of goods, expenses, sales, and cash flow was not as bad as I thought it would be. Joe and I planned a mini retreat to get out of the office and away from distractions to take a look at the business's financial health. I can't say I fully understood it all, but it didn't kill me either." Grace smiled sheepishly.

Janise laughed. "Well, I am so happy to see that it didn't kill you because today, we are going to move on to the next piece of the business suit. Your business's structure is like looking at the construction, fabric, and feel of a quality, custom-made business suit. Ready?"

"Ready!" Grace nodded and picked up her coffee mug to warm her hands while Janise got started.

I don't like the cold weather, Grace grumbled to herself.

"You are in such a niche business. Obviously, a folding carton is not a niche, but the kind of high-end work that you do is most definitely a specialty. As we look at creating a balanced succession plan, it is crucial to look at the strength, structure, and foundation of your business and financials. We will take a deeper look at the numbers that you and Joe worked so hard to compile with this process. Those financials will play a key role as we identify essential areas of growth that will strengthen the structure. Believe it or not, simply analyzing the financial statements could be enough to expose growing cracks in what looks like a good process or department. Looking beyond the gross margins and paying attention to ways to improve cashflow could be the way to prevent an impending and potentially devastating loss. Can you tell me how you evaluate your business and industry growth opportunities when making future projections?"

Still holding her mug, Grace answered, "We are quite involved and active in our industry. We keep a close watch on how various regulations affect all aspects of the corrugated cartons and specialty carton professions. We visit trade shows held in our customers' industries to better determine what they have planned in their future, because their future affects our future. We also keep a close eye on how much artificial intelligence and new technology affect what we do."

"Those are great ways to keep your head in the game. Where would you rank your company against your competition?" Janise was leaning on the right arm of her chair, holding her pen at the ready. Grace could see the edge of the notebook at the bottom of the screen.

"I would say we are one of the top leaders in our industry. Our competition certainly keeps us on our toes and inspires us to keep thinking outside of the box. We have had the honor of winning multiple packaging awards in the recent past, and I think our peers genuinely respect what we do."

"Do you see this as a business that is growing or declining?" Janise asked as she finished jotting her notes down.

"Fortunately, the area that we specialize in is an area that is growing. There is a continuous need for beautiful and functional cartons in several of the industries we cater to. Thanks to the YouTube beauty influencers, the cosmetic industry has seen tremendous growth and is alive and well. Skincare and cosmetics companies are some of our best customers."

"Excellent, and are you scaling to grow along with them? It is crucial to understand your positioning in your industry. After all, as you grow this business, that growth will lead to the company's viability and future salability, which will give you choices. You may also have the opportunity to semi-retire and have the best of both worlds. Do you think this is the type of business that a millennial or Gen Xer would be interested in buying?"

Grace was nodding in agreement as Janise spoke. "Yes, I think so. Although it is hard work, the work that we do has a slightly glamorous appeal. Also, we have made every effort to make sure that the business has environmentally sustainable practices. We know that it is essential to not only Joe and me but to our employees—especially our younger employees."

"Are there a lot of regulatory requirements that you have to adhere to? Do you have a specific team member that stays on top of that?" Janise probed.

"There are some regulations that are especially important to our business. We have both consultants and in-house professionals that keep us abreast of all of the waste requirements, recycling requirements, and more." Grace took a sip of the coffee and waited for the next question.

"In a perfect world, do you see yourself leaving the business?"

"Yes, absolutely! As much as I love this business, I would love to travel and see the world and explore other cultures."

"How old are you in this vision?" Janise scratched another note.

"I've thought that around seventy years old, I may back out and take a more consultant-like approach. My goal is to remain active and contribute as much as I absolutely can. Being useful and having a purpose is critical for me—always has been, and I suspect that won't change after I drop my day-to-day responsibilities here. Now, I do love to travel, and I do have other hobbies, so there may come a time when I want to do more of that and less of this. But for now, this is where I want to be."

"In that future vision, do you see yourself with a business partner?" Janise was leaning forward now, really trying to see Grace's vision.

"If I chose to take on a business partner, I could see myself being in a partnership with Joe."

"Yes, it seems you two already have a good partnership of sorts. Can you tell me a little bit about the retirement plan that you currently have in place?"

Oh, here comes the confusing stuff.

"Yes, we currently have a 401k plan that has been in place for well over twenty years. Some of the employees participate in the plan while others choose not to." Grace took another quick sip of her cooling coffee.

Janise leaned forward a bit more. "Is that a concern for you?"

"Yes, I am often times concerned about the retirement future for my employees, and I'm also concerned about the retirement future for Joe and myself." Grace noticed how furrowed her brow was in the video thumbnail next to Janise's face.

"What do you mean by that?" Janise coaxed.

Grace took a deep breath before diving in. "Well, I look at the economy and what our employees are setting aside for the future. I also recognize that we do not have a pension that provides income to them. Since Social Security may not be enough, that means that my employees will have to rely only on their savings. I don't see them saving as much as they should. If they cannot save enough, they will struggle. That concerns me." Anxiety constricted her chest, and she took a long deep breath before continuing. "Even Joe and I should be setting aside a lot more. We have been penalized in the past for putting too much into the 401k. After all, it is truly designed for our employees and not those of us who are considered 'highly compensated' executives. We were hit pretty hard with a few tax obligations and did not like it at all. We know that there are other options out there, but we simply don't know who to talk to and how to get straight answers."

"Yes, taxes can derail some of the best-laid plans." Janise was shaking her head.

I wonder what she's remembering right now.

Janise visibly dismissed the memories and smiled before continuing. "Although I am not a tax advisor, I think it is important that we all pay our fair share of taxes. I also think you should take advantage of the tax codes written for business owners like yourself. Speaking of tax codes, here's a fun fact: The 401k name comes for the Internal Revenue Code. It is section 401k."

"That is trivia that I can share at my next dinner party." Grace smirked and then they both laughed.

"Yes, you can. The truth is, there are more than ten different retirement plan options available including a few that are 401k plans. They do not all apply to small businesses, but many do. It is important that you know what you want to achieve and are able to articulate your long-term desired outcome to make sure that the proper plan is put in place. Let's add this to the high-priority list of areas to address."

Grace nodded affirmatively. "My fair share. Huh, I like the way that sounds. I would like to find a way to properly plan for retirement—I mean, my next adventure. I do not see myself leaving this business anytime soon. I absolutely love being here and have the energy and visions of taking this company even higher. But, after seeing what happened to my sister…" She felt the exhaustion even more than she heard it in her voice. "The tax and probate bills were sobering, and I can see how unforeseen 'things' happen. Our structure could crumble right before my eyes. Honestly, I want to be here another fifteen years. Since I have no idea what taxes would be at that time, I think I should go on the offense now."

"I agree that offense is the right course. As we look at how your business is structured, we can make sure that you and Joe can adequately set aside monies for your retirement and understand how taxes will affect your retirement."

Grace sighed with some relief. "Yes, that would be very helpful and quite a relief. We don't want to have to depend on selling our business for retirement and then turning over more for taxes than we legally have to."

"Exactly! And that leads me to another question. Let's say you decide that you have had enough and put the business on the market. What happens if the business does not sell?" Janise folded her hands under her chin and waited.

Grace gulped the last of her coffee with Janise's last words. "We have such a great business. I guess we just assume that it will sell. I need to put some thought into that! Quite frankly, it's a terrifying thought!" She set her mug down a little too hard and leaned back into the chair for support.

"Why is it so terrifying?" Janise kept digging.

"Because we have put our blood, sweat, and tears into this business, and we have some amazing employees who deserve the opportunity to continue to work here. If this business goes away, so do their jobs. And that's terrifying!"

"That's a good point. As you envision the silhouette of a well-structured suit, can you see how important it is to address all aspects of your business structure?"

Oh yes, my suit was strong the day of the big sale!

"Yes, I see it." Grace nodded affirmatively.

"Good. Now let's talk about how you show up in the market. Let's move on to marketing." She paused until Grace nodded and then continued, "Do you have a system to identify, describe and price your products and services?"

"We have a super sophisticated software system that keeps track of everything, including raw materials. We also have an extremely qualified team. They keep track of all of our products from inception to distribution. Logistics has become easier and more comfortable with the automation and consolidation of data they share with all of the departments throughout the company."

"I love solid automation. It does make everything easier. What does the pricing look like? Have you been increasing your prices to keep up with inflation?"

"Our pricing is competitive. We stay abreast of what the industry is doing and what our market will bear. We know our prices are a bit higher than the average, but so is our quality. Our customers are satisfied with the services we provide; therefore, we feel our pricing is fair."

"If there were a reduction in business due to some catastrophic event, how would that affect your production and sales?"

Grace sat forward again, leaning her elbows on the desk. "We have a comprehensive emergency contingency plan. I will get a copy for you. But truthfully, it would depend on the type of interruption. Since our business is in California, we have always had an earthquake emergency preparedness procedure. Some of our raw materials come from afar, and we may not get those supplies for months. Fortunately, we maintain a small surplus of certain vital items and machine parts. We are fortunate because we don't live in a region in this country with hurricanes, tornados, or floods every year. Our biggest challenge is keeping everyone focused during those perfect beach or ski days." She laughed at her joke, and Janise laughed along.

"It's tough living in Southern California, isn't it?" Janise teased. "That contingency plan is a good start. I look forward to seeing what you have in place. By adding a succession plan, your emergency preparedness will competently address both the property and the personnel events." Janise took a sip of water from the glass sitting in front of her before continuing. "Okay, let's talk about sales. Have you, in the past, and are you currently keeping track of sales opportunities?"

"Oh yes! We have several sales superstars. They have identified our best referral partners and know exactly the types of opportunities we are looking to pursue. We also use state-of-the-art customer relationship management software, so our sales pipeline is fully automated. This allows our sales team to be proactive at every stage of the sale."

"What is your sales team focused on right now?" Janise asked.

"Customer retention, sales volume, and developing new relationships."

"It sounds like you have a solid structure and team. Do you think there's room for growth in this area?"

"Yes, I think that we can have an even larger and stronger sales team. I would even be willing to have someone come in and coach them because the more they know, the more we can grow. There are a lot of businesses out there waiting for us, and we want to have the manpower to go after new accounts, especially now that our competitors have left some of their customers high and dry."

"That's a great idea. I think I know the right person to help you take your sales to the next level. She's an absolute genius at it. Now, let's move on to branding.

What can you tell me about your brand?" Janise was taking copious notes.

"We have a great brand. We have a lot of history and an excellent reputation, and I love our logo and the high-quality website our team has developed." Grace grinned, satisfied with the great work they had done.

"I agree. Your visual branding is fantastic, which is important for a company known to make such beautiful packaging. Do you think that the brand could be more recognizable?"

"Absolutely, I would like to see a more recognizable national brand. We have some deep industry recognition, but my goal is a presence in the world. After all, it's a global society, right?" Grace beamed as she thought about the brand being known globally.

"Oh yes. Now, more than ever, that is so true. Now, how about advertising? Do you have the advertising budget needed to create a world brand?"

"No, not right now. I guess that's one of my long-term goals. The advertising budget that we have right now is fairly small compared to my vision for the company. We are currently advertising in business-to-business magazines and at conventions, expos, and trade shows. We are clear about who our customers are, and we meet them where they are. As we prepare for our future, we will work to increase our visibility of the brand through advertising. We know the marketing areas in which we get a reasonable rate of return for our efforts. It is about time for us to expand our visibility reach."

"Have you set goals and objectives surrounding your desire to increase your visibility?"

Grace nodded again. "We have had several in-house meetings about where we want to take the company, but we have not hired any outside sources, such as an advertising firm."

"Well, I think once you have a solid plan in place, that kind of investment will make sense. How about operations? I know this is definitely Joe's area of expertise, but can you tell me what you know about it?"

Grace leaned forward. "Joe does his best to keep our leadership team abreast of what is going on in the various departments and projects that he oversees, so I know quite a bit about what he does and how he does it. He maintains relationships with all of our suppliers. He manages the logistics and procedures that affect our manufacturing efforts—all inventory, maintenance, and orders that deal with our equipment and technology needs. He is also dialed into all analytics and how that business activity affects our bottom line. We have seen consistent and tremendous growth due to our internet visibility and growth in our internet store. In fact, we have recently updated our information systems to keep up with the demand and keep us one step ahead of our competition."

"That's fantastic!" Janise exclaimed. "Grace, it looks like your business structure is pretty solid and that there is still some room for growth. I have made a note of several priority areas to address. I will send you over some action items that will help as we look at your business's future.

It is important that you have clear and measurable goals in all aspects of the business."

"Oh, I remember creating SMART goals years ago."

That was very helpful in getting the business on track and operating smoothly again after Dad passed.

"Good, because that is what you need to do again. We talked about your vision of retirement and travel, your quest for a global presence, and some key opportunities to build your brand. So, now it's time to ask how you are going to get there. Your goals need to be specific, measurable, attainable, realistic, and timely. By adding a clear road map in all areas, we will not lose sight of the ultimate goals."

"Got it. My team and I will get started on compiling and clarifying. I am actually looking forward to dreaming big. Let's put our next meeting on the calendar for four weeks from today. This deadline will help us maintain our momentum."

"Sounds good to me!" Janise said as she updated her meeting calendar. "Done. I will see you in four short weeks."

Prepare to Leave In Style at:
www.LeavingInStyle.com/Resources

Chapter Four

CREATE CONFIDENCE
WITH COMPOSURE

"HI, JANISE!" GRACE exclaimed when her face popped onto the screen.

"Good morning, Grace," she replied. "How's your month been?"

"It has actually been fun!" she answered cheerily.

"Great! Tell me more." Janise leaned in to listen.

"The task of looking at my future and creating a realistic timeline was initially scary. However, once I started writing down all of the things I would like to do and places I'd like to go, I really started getting into the process. I let my imagination take me all over the world."

"How did it feel going on that journey?" Janise asked.

"In some ways, it was freeing. In other ways, it made me want to take better care of my business and myself. When I saw myself traveling the world, I saw an energetic and vibrant person who was physically able to have adventures and help other women in business as a mentor."

"Oh yes, we have to take care of ourselves now, so we have that energy and capacity later." Janise agreed. "Did those visions help to come up with a clear exit date?"

"They did. I wrote them all down; and as you suggested, I began to reverse-engineer an exit that will not put the business in peril. Believe it or not, my exit timeline helped me to better understand what we need to build this business and team to the point that I do not need to be here daily. Those building blocks include marketing, advertising, and education. I think I am on the right track."

"Well, that sounds like it was a productive assignment! If you send me your findings, I'll add that into the master plan document I'm developing for you."

"Of course. I'll send it right after we're done here today. What part of the suit are we talking about today?" Grace quipped wryly.

Janise grinned, appreciating how quickly Grace was grasping the fashion framework. "Well, let's see. Today what we're talking about is more about the attitude the suit helps you to experience. Remember showing up to that very first important meeting, with everything accurate and in order and nerves on edge?"

Grace nodded as her body remembered it all. Constricted chest. Busy butterflies in her belly. A ridiculously tight grip on the door handle.

"What did you do to get through that moment—to compose yourself?" Janise asked.

"I took a deep breath, recited a few affirmations, and said, 'I've got this.' I know that everything is in order, and all bases have been covered."

"Right! And with that regained composure, you were ready to step into the meeting with confidence and nail that presentation."

"Oh yeah. I nailed it!" Suddenly, all of the anxious feelings were replaced with those of satisfaction and joy of a job well done.

I felt like I made my dad proud that day. Even though he wasn't in the room, I hope he was looking on and clapping with the rest of them.

"Well, as I'm sure you've experienced since that day, it's tough to operate with that type of confidence when you know you don't have all of the bases covered and everything in proper order. I find that most business owners are extremely knowledgeable about their particular industry and trade practices. Still, they are usually unaware of some of the business practices and preparations that would increase their confidence in their business's solidity and lasting power. There is a vivid example that I just witnessed."

Grace picked up her warm cup of coffee and sat back in her chair.

I love morning meetings over coffee.

"Recently, I attended an introductory membership meeting full of successful young entrepreneurs. They listened intensely to Mark Reyes, a business consultant who shared how he took his business from startup to $170 million by using a Small Business Administration (SBA) loan. After several good years of steady growth, he and his partner decided to sell. Mark discussed the systems he and his partner put into place. Their system allowed him to work considerably less in the business and delve into his hobby and dream of helping others by becoming an angel investor."

Oooh, that does sound like fun!

"In his absence, the business grew beyond his expectations. He acknowledged that the leadership and the proper team made all the difference. Mark talked about understanding the company's value and working with his business partner. He then asked the audience how many of them were in a partnership. About eight business owners raised their hands. Of those who raised their hand, he asked how many of them had a Buy-Sell agreement."

A what kind of agreement? I've never even heard of that before.

"Only three people kept their hands in the air, and he told the others who had put their hands down that they needed to make this agreement a priority. You could feel the confusion and anxiety in the room. The looks of bewilderment on their faces told the truth—they had no idea what a Buy-Sell agreement is, where to get it, nor who to talk to in order to get it. Of course, he didn't share that information during the meeting because that wasn't his point. As I walked out of the conference with my friend, who is a commercial banking president, I asked him if he thought any of those business owners knew what a Buy-Sell agreement is. He agreed that most of them had no clue."

Well, I'm glad I'm not the only clueless one!

"Just because someone is ultra-successful in business, and knows everything about their respective field, does not mean they know all things about the company and the nuances in the areas of expertise that support their business. How about you? Do you know what a Buy-Sell agreement is?" she asked Grace, leaning forward on her desk.

"Honestly, no. It sounds like some type of plan that you put in place to buy and sell businesses; I have never heard of this type of contract, nor do I know of anyone who has one."

"A Buy-Sell Agreement is a contract written by an attorney that spells out what is to happen in business should a triggering event occur," Janise started.

"Triggering events?" Grace asked while Janise took a sip of her tea.

"Yes, a triggering event."

"So, it is not for buying and selling a business? I am confused." Grace set her coffee down and picked up her pen and notepad. She was definitely going to have to take some notes on this one.

"The term Buy-Sell Agreement is often confusing to the nonlegal individual hearing the term for the first time. Think of a Buy-Sell Agreement as the legal definition for a 'Business Pre-Nup.'"

"Oh! Right! I know what a pre-nup is." Grace nodded and checked to make sure she was right about where this was going. "I started to wonder if this pre-nup would also work with shareholders?"

"Yes! It is the type of contract on the 'must have' list if you have a business partner or shareholders. The business pre-nup is best written when all parties are cooperating and agree as to what is in the best interest of the business should a triggering event occur. As the sole shareholder, with an 'heir apparent,' you can have a one-way Buy-Sell agreement."

"Is this something that might be covered in our bylaws? I know there is a little bit of language that kind of makes me think the bylaws address this type of scenario." Grace was excited about where this was going.

"That is a common thought. There are many business owners who genuinely believe that everything is covered in the bylaws alone, as if they are the succession plan. While there may be circumstances addressed in the bylaws, the bylaws are not a funding source."

"What do you mean by funding source?" Grace asked.

Wow, I'm surprised I've never heard about any of this before.

"Let's explore some of the areas covered in a 'Business Pre-Nup' and then we'll circle back to funding sources."

Grace nodded and held her pen at the ready. "I'm listening."

"Buy-Sell Agreements are usually written by attorneys who specialize in contracts and business. Some Estate Planning Attorneys will also write the agreement because the consequences can affect the shareholders' estate. It's also important to include a whole team of advisors, which you'll understand as we explore this. But first, let's look at some of the most common triggers in a Buy-Sell Agreement. Since many of the most common triggers can begin with a letter D, I have affectionately named these explanations 'D Day.'"

"'D' day? Well, let's hope we don't have to go to war over these!" It was a half-joke. Grace started to feel pretty stressed about these triggering events, and she didn't even know what they were yet.

"That's exactly what a pre-nup of any sort is for, right? We write everything down ahead of time so that we don't have to go to war when something happens. Let's look at them:

Disability

"When we talk about disability, we're not talking about a broken arm or leg, resulting in you being out of work for a month or six weeks. We are talking about a disability that can keep you out of work for more than one year or forever. Even though the average disability claim is nine months, I want you to think more along the lines of chronic illness and catastrophic illnesses or injuries. Some that come to mind are multiple sclerosis, heart attack, stroke, Parkinson's…"

"Or cancer," Grace added to complete the thought. "Watching my sister's struggle was certainly a wakeup call."

"Yes, as you can see and have experienced, we all know someone who has been afflicted by one of these terrible illnesses, and they, too, were once in the workplace. For many, the disability may require extensive rehabilitation, or they may not recover to the point where returning to work is an option. For those fortunate enough to work through extensive rehabilitation, life is still entirely different and may turn out to be more of a challenge than one can handle. But the most important point here is that when someone is disabled, his or her bills don't just disappear. In fact, the expenses are typically increasing."

"You're absolutely right. And the cost of drugs alone can simply break the bank." Grace's heart felt heavy as she remembered how many thousands of dollars her sister spent on meds that didn't cure her.

"Yes, and then we have to look at what happens to the business in their absence. Most companies cannot afford to continue to pay an income to someone who is not working. If that person happens to be the one generating the sales, this creates a double hit on the business. As a business owner, a key person, or partner, the knowledge and skills that this individual brings to the business will be missed and need to be replaced as soon as possible."

"Absolutely." Grace took a deep breath as she thought about what might happen at the business if something happened to her.

"When someone dies, we know what death is, what it looks like, and acknowledge that it is permanent; but when it comes to a disability, severe injury, or extended illness, there is no 'poster child' for what that looks like. If you are too sick or injured to come to work, some tough questions must be asked and answered: How long can the business continue to function without its leader or a part of the leadership team? What happens if a key executive becomes that disabled person? How long can the company afford to pay them without them being productive? Is that payment legal? After all, it's not truly earned income."

"Whew. Those are some tough questions." Grace sighed.

"Yes, ma'am. But you can see how having answers to them *before* something happens would give everyone a sense of security should a disability occur." When she saw Grace nod, Janise continued. "Let's talk about the next D: Disease."

Disease

"Disabilities can come from a variety of circumstances and result in varying obstacles. Think about the challenges that come with cystic fibrosis, sickle-cell anemia, or Huntington's disease, all of which are hereditary. Or it can be something acquired such as Lyme disease, bacterial meningitis, or West Nile virus."

"I have seen some extreme and devastating illnesses. I know someone who nearly died and lost his ability to walk after something as simple as a mosquito bite. Since he was an employee, I had not clearly thought about how that would affect a business if it had been the owner."

"A mosquito bite?!? That is so frightening. Was he able to continue working?" Janise asked.

"Not right away. After being in and out of the hospital for more than a year, he went to physical therapy and progressed to being able to sit in a wheelchair. When he attempted to go back to work in a different role, it was simply too taxing on his body. He no longer had the stamina to maintain his position and ultimately had to retire. He is still a young man who has a lot of ambition and had a lot of professional goals, but now his full-time job is getting healthy."

"That is an excellent example of what happens daily. The next D may affect those who are a bit closer to retirement, but that is not always the case."

Dementia (mental incompetence)

"The use of the term may seem like a stretch, but it perfectly illustrates the fact that mental capacity can diminish over time. This is a real scenario that is played out more often now that we are living longer and working at older ages. Even in the last United States Presidential campaign, the top three front-running candidates were 69 years old, 70 years old, and 75 years old, respectively. I am not implying that they have limited mental capacity, just illustrating how our society's seniors are still productive and often working in vital leadership positions within a company."

"Yes, I know that issue was voiced several times. Older often means wiser, but it also means they are more susceptible to memory loss and diminished capacity," Grace affirmed.

"Exactly. With aging comes a greater likelihood of ailments and potentially a decline in mental ability that may interfere with daily duties and decision-making. According to the Alzheimer's Association, more than **one in nine (11.3%) Americans over the age of 65 has Alzheimer's dementia.** In the case of a business, a decision must be made as to how that person will exit the business. Just because someone is no longer able to work, they still may deserve to receive compensation and an option to sell shares at the predetermined rate."

"It would certainly be heartbreaking and challenging to figure out how to provide an income to someone leaving a position of such importance, knowing they no longer have what it takes to do a job properly." Grace grimaced at the memory of a few examples of her colleagues facing this challenge.

"Yes, but if they're not removed, they could wreak havoc on the productivity and stability of a business." Janise paused and asked, "Can you guess what the next D might be?"

Grace reflected for a few moments. "Divorce?"

"You're so good, Grace!"

"Well, I've seen some things," she said, shaking her head at some of the memories of messy divorces she'd witnessed over the years.

Divorce

"Oh yeah. Me, too," Janise started. "Love is emotional and an affair of the heart. In stark contrast, divorce is less about love and more about business. Most people do not marry planning to get a divorce, and their business partners surely do not want to be a part of this kind of personal drama. We have all seen amicable divorces and those that are quite acrimonious. Of course, it's the latter one that causes the most problems in business, especially when there are business partners."

"Oh yes, I've seen divorce take down an entire business," Grace confirmed.

"Right. And since more than half of the marriages end in divorce, this is a conversation that must be addressed in the event of relationship dissolution. If there is no Buy-Sell Agreement in place that addresses what will happen in the business if one of the shareholders gets a divorce, the business can find itself with an unintended business owner. And, unfortunately, this new partner may not want to see the company grow and prosper. I spoke with a business owner who said that when his business partner got a divorce, the ex-wife became an 'active' business partner because she was awarded shares of the business as a part of her divorce settlement."

Grace leaned forward. *I haven't heard one like this!*

"She never had a real interest in the business, nor did she particularly care for the business partner. What she wanted was to be bought out at a higher price than what was offered. As a result, every time someone from the business would contact her for a decision or request document signatures, she would delay the process and refuse to return their phone calls. This, of course, made the daily activities of doing business stressful and complicated. Although the partners thought their bylaws covered everything, there was no discussion or provisions as to what to do with a hostile or unwanted business partner."

"Ugh, that's terrible!" Grace exclaimed.

"I agree! Remember the famous case of Anthony Maglica and his partner Claire Halasz? Anthony is the owner and the founder of Maglite flashlights, which are quite popular and used mainly by law enforcement agencies. The divorce resulted in ridiculous amounts of litigation, a huge payout to Claire, and workplace distress when employees took sides. When the divorce is public, employees and others may take sides or even undermine or derail the business to show support for the side with whom they have chosen to align themselves."

"Oh, my goodness, how awful!" Grace could hardly believe what she was hearing.

"When there's not a plan in writing, a business owner can find themselves with business partners that they never would choose to work with. It might not be the future ex-wife of a business partner; it may be a competitor. Suppose there is nothing in writing that addresses how the shares are sold. In that case, a shareholder could become angry with the business owner and sell their shares to the competition.[1]"

"Wow, that would be horrible!" Grace shook her head at the possibility.

"It is. The Business Pre-Nup also addresses the first right of refusal challenges. If a business partner dies, his heirs may want to or insist on selling to a buyer of their choice. The first right of refusal could prevent those shares from landing in the hands of their fiercest competitor. Through industry gossip, the competition is also aware of what is going on. I know of a situation where the competing firm reached out to the employees and offered them jobs. Can you imagine? The employees quickly responded because they were so unsure of what would happen, and they had financial obligations to honor. When the employees left, they took the customer relationships with them. After all, the customers still had business needs. Since there was no structure nor documentation, the estate or the value of that business went from potentially viable to almost zero overnight. This became

1   Anthony Maglica. (2021). In Wikipedia. https://en.wikipedia.org/w/index. php?title=Anthony_Maglica&oldid=1043281821

the legacy left to the owner's son: no business, no life insurance, and no inheritance from that business."

Grace was speechless.

"Although the situation is unlikely for you right now since you are not married and do not have any partners, it's important to know what is possible, especially if you decide to marry in the future or change your business relationship with Joe. In order to keep divorce and other issues out of your business, it would be good to have a conversation with your attorney. Especially in this lovely state of ours." Janise's smile showed tinges of sarcasm.

"Especially in our state?" Grace asked.

"Yes, since California is a community property state, the business partners and their spouses must all sign the Buy-Sell agreement drawn up by your attorney." Janise paused to make sure Grace was following and then continued, "Let's move on to the next D."

Departure (fired, quit, retired)

"A shareholder's departure can disrupt the workplace. If it is an abrupt departure, such as being fired or quitting, there needs to be a strategy that will reduce the amount of potential litigation. Will there be a severance package? How will the leaders communicate about the departure with the rest of the employees? And so on."

"I have seen and heard about these types of departures, and they are often not pretty," Grace interjected.

"Not even the retirements?" Janise asked.

"Nope. Not even the retirements. In one case, a senior executive was retiring and did not get the clean and clear compensation package he thought he would receive. He expected twice the monthly income he actually received and was so angry that he threatened to sue the remaining partners. They showed him the books, and due to the great recession of 2008, they had not fully recovered and did not have the cash on hand to address his needs. It was all so confusing to me." Grace wrapped her hands around her warm mug of coffee.

"Oh, I'm sure it was just as confusing to them," Janise mused.

"It was. They admired and respected their former partner but simply did not have the sales and income to meet his demands."

"Of course, they did not know any better, but they could have put together some nice retirement options that would have made everyone happy, especially if he had given them fair warning of his goals and desire to retire."

"Yes, he had been talking about retiring since I met him. So, I would say they had plenty of time."

"Grace, it's also important to think about, not just the amount, but the timing of payments. A business can determine if the retirement would pay out a lump sum to the retiree or create some type of annuity where payments are paid overtime."

"I definitely want to know more about how this works, especially in a scenario like mine where I am currently the sole shareholder." Grace made herself a note to dig into this more later.

"We will definitely make sure you have peace of mind with your options and decisions when it comes to retiring. Let's move on to the next D—debt."

Debt (Bankruptcy)

"When a shareholder is seeking bankruptcy protection from creditors, one of the requirements is to list all creditors and all assets. Of course, one of the assets will include shares of the business. If the courts require that asset to be sold, and there is no first right of refusal in place, the share can be purchased by anyone, including a competitor."

"Good to know! I'm going to get a list of all of these, right?" Grace was becoming more and more determined to address all of these potential D-Days.

"Oh yes, I'll send a list for you to review and jot some notes on before you work directly with an attorney to create the agreement." When Grace exhaled, she continued, "Let's move on to the next D."

Disqualification (Loss of Professional Licenses)

"Any business professional who is required to have an active license, certification, education, or designation in good standing runs the risk of losing everything if they are suspended, terminated, or lose that career. For example, attorneys, contractors, dentists, doctors, real estate brokers, insurance professionals, financial advisors, etc. have suppliers and contracts that rely on them having a certain quality standard such as ISO 9001 certifications or maybe a Women Business Enterprise (WBE), which helps them meet some internal business goals. I think this last certification applies to you, right?"

Grace nodded.

"What if something goes wrong quality-wise, and you lose your certification, or your female majority owner is no longer a part of the business. What provisions do you have to address these issues?"

"Not only could that hurt our business if we're attempting to sell, but this could also limit our pool of qualified buyers." Grace saw where this was going.

"Right, and what happens to those customers?" Janise pushed.

"That's a tough one because the first thing that comes to mind is that our closest competitor will benefit from our lack of planning."

"Exactly! Time for a business pre-nup."

Wow, I'm so glad we're doing this!

"Ready for the next D?"

Dissolution of Partnership and Disagreement (Bad Business Partners)

"Have you ever heard the stories of the great friends who get together for drinks and come up with the best business idea that is going to change the world?" Janise asked.

"Oh yes, plenty of times. I've had colleagues come up with some innovative relationships this way," Grace answered, several instances crossing her mind.

"So, you know how this story usually goes. The friends pencil out an idea on a napkin, and they start putting a plan in place that is undoubtedly going to make them rich, rich, rich! The new business gets going, and there is a lot of work and progress taking place. Everything seems to be moving along well for a few years. But then, over time, one partner begins to realize that he is working in the business more than his old friend. The old friend has become an absentee owner who is combative and just will not carry his weight. They begin arguing and fighting over some of the most mundane issues about the business's growth and productivity and eventually decide that one of them must go. Since the old friend is out of touch and certainly does not want to work, he agrees to sell his portion to the active partner."

"Yep, I've seen that story a few times… and not just in movies!" Grace exclaimed.

Janise laughed. "Me, too. Businesses are like marriages. There are a lot of ups and downs and hard work that must go into nurturing and growing. In this case, it just may be time for a business divorce. The partners will trigger the business pre-nup and begin working with their advisors to make a smooth transition. However, when there is no provision to address how a partnership can transition, this could become a major issue when determining how the firm's assets and liabilities must be handled.

Delinquency (Arrest)

Janise continued, "Okay, using the term Delinquency may be a stretch, but it illustrates what can happen on 'D Day.' The arrest of a shareholder could be minor, or it could turn into a life-changing event. If the shareholder's situation could potentially cause harm to the business, a legal provision clause may keep a business from being dragged into a situation that is far beyond its control."

"Yeah, I'm aware of several companies who have had to deal with these types of events, but I've never thought about what I would do in that situation," Grace answered honestly.

"Well, you hire quality people, and so it probably just would not occur to you. No one thinks this could happen, but it does—infractions from multiple Driving While Intoxicated arrests to trouble due to moral improprieties, embezzlement, or worse. As a business owner, the last thing you want to do is have to hire a lawyer and fight in court to protect your business from the illegal actions of others. And now for the D that you're probably most familiar with due to recent events."

Grace's heart dropped a little, but she took a deep breath and nodded to say she was ready.

Death

"As you know from experience, when a vital member or key person dies, there is a void left both professionally and personally. When that professional is a viable participant in that business, it does not matter how sick or old they are; we always deem that loss an untimely death."

It's always too soon for those of us left behind.

"You also saw how the death of a key person can also cause concern and a ripple effect throughout the lives of their employees who begin to fear for the stability of their jobs. Even suppliers can become concerned about the risk of continued business and accounts being paid promptly."

"Yes, I've seen it," Grace commented.

"So, to address this certainty of mortality, a proactive conversation that includes who will run the business is necessary. Should the decision be to sell the business, the immediate strategy would be to stabilize operations, designate a temporary leader, or engage an executive search firm to secure an interim leader. It is challenging for most business owners to discuss and plan for their inevitable demise; so tricky, in fact, that most business owners do not have the conversation at all."

"Yeah, well, without having seen what happened with my sister, I'm not sure I would be aware of the need for this conversation, let alone be willing to have it." Grace shook her head.

"Right. And you saw what happened with Paula's employees, too. As much as one's employees may like their job and their employer, they immediately want to know what will happen to them. The livelihood of their families depends on the company's next move. Even the most loyal employees may think about looking for a job elsewhere to avoid watching the business decline or being blindsided with a layoff or business closure. No matter how much they want to stay, their mortgage, car note, and childcare must still be paid."

"Yes, I saw how hard it was for some of her employees to choose their own self-preservation over loyalty to the business. I couldn't blame them at all."

"Right, and suppliers and customers will want to know and have the assurance that they can continue to rely on your company to fulfill all outstanding orders and contracts. As much as they may enjoy having you as a supplier, it is business, after all. If they must bring in another supplier to meet their needs and ultimately keep their customers happy, most will not hesitate to do so."

"Again, makes perfect sense," Grace responded, unable to hide the sadness.

"When it comes to the loss of leadership, lenders may also become a little skittish. The banker and banking relationship that your business has come to rely on may be taken out of your trusted banker's hands and moved to the risk portfolio and reviewed. Worst case, the bank has the right to call the loan because of the increased risk, as the funding provided was likely secured by the knowledge and expertise of the now-deceased owner or key executive."

"Ah, now I understand 'funding sources.'" Grace jotted a quick note on her notepad.

"Exactly. So, at this point, the business has lost both its leadership and the funding put in place to help grow the business. These circumstances can cause an avalanche effect that can derail the best of businesses. When there is nothing in writing, the government always has a solution for you. Unfortunately, in most states, your heirs and business partners may find themselves in probate court." She paused. "Grace, how about we take a quick five-minute break? I know this conversation is lengthy, and that last bit probably brought up some tough memories and emotions. Let's do a quick reset. Sound good?"

"Yes, thank you." Grace muted her microphone, turned off her video, and made a beeline for the door.

Some sunshine ought to help me shake this off.

A Supplier's Prospective

Five minutes later, Grace was feeling revived as she unmuted and turned on her video. Janise was there, waiting for her. "Thanks, Janise. I needed some sunshine."

"Ah yes. That vitamin D is so helpful."

"While I was out there, I was wondering about the suppliers part of our conversation. How would suppliers know whether we have a succession plan or not?" Grace asked.

"Good question. While attending an annual Women Business Enterprise National Council's (WBENC) National convention last year, I spoke with a gentleman, Terry, who told me he was the Supplier Diversity Manager for a billion-dollar manufacturing enterprise. His job is to award supplier contracts on a large scale. After I explained how I assist business owners, Terry proceeded to tell me a story about one of his suppliers, who was awarded such a large contract that his employer required that the supplier have a succession plan on file. They wanted peace of mind in knowing that if something happened to one of the core leaders, the contract could and would still be fulfilled."

"Oh, so maybe they ask for it when the contract is sizable enough, or if they have learned a hard lesson by experience," Grace mused out loud.

Janise nodded. "Exactly. And in this case, the supplier procrastinated and was not happy with this new demand. He had worked with the manufacturer for years, and he felt the manufacturer was trying to tell him how to run his business. Terry told me that he had to meet with the supplier's executive team and explain that they would rescind the contract if they did not put a plan in place. That this wasn't about telling them how to run their business. They were awarding this supplier a huge contract, making them an integral part of their own business's ability to meet their customers' needs. As a part of their due diligence, they needed to make sure that this contract would be fulfilled in the case that something happened to the supplier's leadership. After he explained the additional benefits of a succession plan, which we have covered today, the owner immediately put one in place."

"This is excellent information for me. What happens when a business owner doesn't have a partner or spouse to come in and take over?" Grace asked.

One Way Buy-Sell Agreement

"That's a great question. Just because a business owner doesn't have a partner or a spouse doesn't mean that their business isn't worthy of continuing. Let's say that a sole business owner has a dedicated employee who would make a fantastic owner. Still, she doesn't have enough money for a down payment to purchase the business in the future. The owner can set up a One-Way Buy-Sell Agreement, a safe way to transfer one's interest in the business. With a One-Way Buy-Sell Agreement, the key person has the first right of refusal option when the business owner decides to sell or a triggering event transpires. This contract is also a way that you can minimize any interference from other family members, spouses, and children."

Grace nodded. "Yes, I can see how that would be a major benefit for some business owners. How are these types of contracts set up?"

"There are several ways to set them up. We look at the overall business, the number of partners or shareholders included, and the desired outcome. Since all these options have legal and tax advantages and disadvantages, it is vital to consider and address them after the overall business assessment." Janise shared her screen to begin discussing the various options.

The Construction Options for A Buy-Sell Agreement

Cross-Purchase Agreement

"This is also known as a Stockholder Purchase or an agreement that takes place between partners or shareholders. This agreement spells out that in the event of a transfer of ownership, the company owners will have the first option to purchase the business interests. This is the most common of the three options.

Entity Purchase Agreement

"This is also known as a Stock Redemption, which means that the business will buy back all of the company shares. This agreement is beneficial when the business is larger and there are more than three shareholders or interested parties.

Hybrid Agreement
(also known as the "Wait and See" option)

"This one is a combination of a cross-purchase agreement and an entity purchase agreement. When there is an owner who is leaving the business, she can give the company the option to purchase her shares. Suppose the company is not willing to buy her shares. In that case, other shareholders or an outside individual or entity will have the option to purchase them. The owner can also do it the other way around, which means that she can first offer her shares to her fellow business partners or shareholders. If the business partners choose not to buy them, she can then offer to sell her shares back to the business."

"Well, I can see how it got its name: 'Wait and See,'" Grace reasoned.

"Yes, you are right. In some cases, there are other options or scenarios possible, so it is important to seek the advice of the attorney who will be drafting the loan documents. So, now let's talk about funding options."

Grace kept her pen on the notepad and was ready to take some furious notes.

Buy-Sell Agreement Funding Options

"As I shared earlier, when introducing the concept of a Buy-Sell agreement, business owners usually say they have provisions in their bylaws as to how they will handle the business in the event one of them dies. Well, determining how you handle business is one thing; having the money needed to support that decision is another. Think of it this way: it is like creating a living trust for your family and never taking steps to designate nor place the property in the trust. There are a multitude of ways to fund the Buy-Sell agreement. Each has its advantages and disadvantages. Let's look at the most common funding options:

Bank Loan

"If the bank is comfortable with the business model for continuation and leadership, an existing line of credit or bank loan may be used to buy time for the business. However, since the company has lost a vital individual with core competency, the bank may not feel comfortable lending money in an unstable environment.

Cash

"Keeping a lump sum of money readily available to be paid to the heirs in exchange for shares is an option but not so practical. Since the Buy-Sell agreement may require the shares to be purchased, the triggering event may happen when there is not enough cash on hand to complete the transaction. The surplus cash in the business can be used to purchase outstanding shares. As with the 'sinking fund,' the same disadvantage exists. We will discuss the sinking fund a little more in a moment.

Insurance

"One of the least expensive and the most practical ways that most people fund a Buy-Sell agreement is the use of life insurance and disability insurance. Life Insurance is the most common way business owners fund Buy-Sell agreements because it is also one of the most cost-effective ways. One of the advantages of using Life Insurance is that it is what we call self-completing. This means once you have purchased the coverage, the required amount is immediately available in the event one of the leaders dies unexpectedly."

"I see," Grace said aloud as she continued to take notes.

"When set up properly, the death benefit is income tax-free. Depending on the type of insurance used, there may also be tax-advantaged access if it has cash. When you are using permanent insurance, it can strengthen the company's business assets. One of the disadvantages to deciding to use Life Insurance is that you must qualify for the coverage. Some things taken into consideration are your age, health, occupation, and lifestyle. Are you a smoker or a non-smoker? What are your hobbies? Are they risky or dangerous? For some large corporations, the policy's cash value may trigger an alternative minimum tax. Unfortunately, not everyone is eligible for this option. Before implementing a contract that is based on life insurance coverage, it is essential that you first determine insurability."

"Makes sense," Grace agreed.

Disability Buy-out

"There is another type of protection to think about. Most business owners understand the importance and need for a Buy-Sell agreement in the event of death and include life insurance to fund their agreement, but what they do not realize is that we are 25% more likely to become disabled before we retire. As we discussed earlier, disability has no 'poster child.' It does not look the same for everyone. There are countless ways to become disabled, and that disability can be an extended disability or permanent disability. Think of the effects of a heart attack, stroke, Parkinson's, multiple sclerosis, or brain injury."

"Yes, I've seen some business owners deal with disability. It's so sad to see them forced to walk away from a business that they have built with their own hands."

"Yes, but just because he steps away from the business does not mean he no longer needs income or that the business can afford to pay him while he has this extended or permanent absence, right?"

"Right," Grace agreed.

"There may come the point when that business owner needs to be bought out, and that is when disability buy-out insurance is a practical and viable option. Without a disability buy-out in place, a disabled business owner would continue to take his salary. As you could imagine, if you were disabled, the effects on your business could be devastating. All of the roles and responsibilities still need to be addressed, and the business could decline without your leadership. In the best interest of all parties, you can have a clause with a buy-out option after a certain period. This timeframe is determined by the insurance company that will be making the payments."

"Oh, I guess that makes sense," Grace said, tapping her pen against her chin.

"During a training session with a few colleagues, we studied the consequences of a physicians' group that prepared a Buy-Sell Agreement by consulting only with their attorney. The contract drafted stated that should any of the doctors become disabled, they would convene, validate the permanent disability of the ill partner, and then begin the buy-out process. Once the agreement was completed, they contacted their insurance professional and explained what they wanted but could not find an insurance company that would buy into their legal scheme. After being educated on the process, the agreement had to be amended."

Grace set her pen down for a minute.

"Had the insurance professional been included in the preliminary stages of the plan, his expertise would have saved them a lot of time, money, and hassle. If an insurance company is going to fund the buy-out, they will also require their staff doctors to review the circumstances of the case and make the final decision and then (usually) pay the disabled owner over a three to five-year time by way of installments. There are some insurance companies that will pay a lump sum of the predetermined buy-out amount. We can discuss this further later."

"Wow," Grace interjected. "I can see how this would release the company from paying a highly-compensated executive who is unable to perform his or her duties and use the cash flow and savings to continue growing the business." It was all starting to make sense.

"Yes, and one of the benefits of a Disability Buyout is the option to have a predetermined sell amount for your share of the business should you need it. Premiums are not deductible, and the Internal Revenue Service requires that you pay taxes on one side of the transaction. In this case, the monies received are not treated as taxable income when you file a disability claim."

"Since we would have to pay taxes one way or the other, I think I would want to pay as little as is legally required," Grace surmised.

"Exactly! If you pay taxes on the premium, it is like paying taxes on the seed instead of the harvest. This type of coverage can also replace a portion of earned income, including bonuses. There are also disability options that will cover outstanding bank loans if necessary. This is ideal when a collateral assignment is required for a loan. Considering this type of coverage is for a disability, there is a good chance you will need and use some of the disbursements to pay for health-related costs such as deductibles, co-pays, non-formulary medications, and experimental treatments."

"Oh yes, there are so many little expenses that pop up to surprise you!" Grace shook her head, trying to dislodge the memories of her sister's medical expenses.

"Yes, and when a business owner becomes disabled, the accumulation of your retirement plan, savings, and investments also usually stop. Like other inconveniences in life, there can be unforeseen expenses incurred due to or after injury or disability. Both the life insurance and disability buy-out can free up monies that can be used to engage an executive search to locate a qualified replacement and fill the intellectual gap so the business can continue."

"Oh yes, what a great idea!"

Promissory Notes (Installment Payments)

"Installment payments are a great way to transfer the business with payment terms. It is also lovely because those terms will not deplete the cash reserves and do allow for smaller payments over an extended period of months or years. The interest rates may also be deductible with this type of repayment option. It is crucial that you discuss this with your accountant because there are several disadvantages when buying shares with a promissory note. The interest may be added to the buy-out price of the business."

Grace cocked her head to one side, letting Janise know that she needed additional information.

"When a promissory note is written, it is done so with the greatest intentions of picking up and continuing to run a very successful business. This is more of a 'plan for the best and expect the best' as opposed to a 'plan for the worst and expect the best' plan. In this case, the conditions and note payments are only as good as the new leader's ability to grow the business and the cash flow that accompanies said growth. Currently, there is a potentially high default risk with this type of agreement. The business can go under, be dissolved, or file for bankruptcy protection. In either of these scenarios, the promissory note would never be satisfied.

Inflations may also work against the transaction. A promissory note may be based on a low value, an unrealistic interest rate, and or a payment schedule. If the value is not regularly addressed, the note may be based on an under or overpayment for shares."

"That doesn't sound like a great option." Grace scrunched her nose up.

"Yeah, definitely not one of my regular recommendations."

Sinking Fund

"The sinking fund is a set of earnings put aside each year to fund a transaction. The sinking fund will allow the company to provide a lump sum for the purchase of shares promptly. Accumulating large amounts of cash can also be difficult. One disadvantage is that it is impossible to predict when you will need these funds. If you have not amassed what is required to purchase outstanding shares, this deficit could create a legal issue."

"Yeah, I now understand the 'sinking' term."

"There is a high opportunity cost because that money which is set aside is not being used to help expand and grow the business. If there is a shortfall in the sinking fund, the cash flow may become the next casualty. To fully fund an account like this, you must accumulate after-tax dollars, and it may take months or years to do so."

"I don't think I'm interested in this option either," Grace offered. "This might be the toughest part of my planning."

"Why is that?" Janise probed.

"Because I actually have to take a serious look at my own life and the likelihood of becoming disabled or dying. Who wants to go on that journey?" Grace asked rhetorically.

"Not too many people want to think about these topics, let alone plan for them. I can assure you—you will feel so much better after putting a safety net in place."

"I guess you're right."

"I am, Grace. In this instance, I have a feeling you will thank me later. I would like you to collect your thoughts in each area to be prepared to speak with your attorney. It will help you make the most of your time."

"Okay, I will work on this over the next month. Thank you, Janise."

"My pleasure. I'll see you at the same time next month?" she asked.

"Yes, see you then."

Prepare to Leave In Style at:
www.LeavingInStyle.com/Resources

Chapter Five

STEP IN STYLE THROUGH THE TRANSITION

CLICKING THE BUTTON to join the meeting, Grace noticed how eager she was for this next conversation with Janise. *I am learning so much, and I already feel so much better about my future.*

"Hi, Grace! How are you?" Janise's smile lit up the screen in front of her.

"I was thinking about how grateful I am to have you on my team, Janise. I'm already feeling better about the future of this business."

"Well, I'm definitely as grateful to be able to help," Janise started. "And with all of the conversations and planning that we have done to build a strong foundation for the future of the business, Grace, there are no guarantees in what the future holds."

"Oh yes. I know that we cannot predict the future." Grace nodded as memories of life's curveballs floated across her mind.

"Well, there is one guarantee: The one thing that I can guarantee is that you will leave this business. We all have the same guarantee. One of my biggest challenges is getting business owners to recognize and acknowledge that guarantee and plan for it as much as possible."

"Ugh. You're right. We don't want to deal with our mortality," Grace mused.

"Nor the possibility of morbidity. Remember what I said earlier: We have a greater chance of becoming disabled before we die, and we should plan accordingly.

"You are so right, Janise. You would be so proud of me. After the phlebotomist came to my home to complete my mini medical exam and my morning meditation last Saturday, I sat down and did just that."

"Just what?" she prompted.

"I thought about my life, health, and non-health-related things that can happen to shorten our life expectancy. It was so surreal. But in doing my assignment, I did have a sense of peace come over me. The best way to explain it is like having a sense of calm after taking a self-defense class. Suddenly, you know how to protect yourself. I know it's a strange analogy, but that's what comes to mind."

"You're right, Grace. I am proud of you. That is a huge milestone. It's those baby steps that will get us to the finish line. Speaking of baby steps, tell me, how did your insurance physical go?"

"It was interesting. There was a very kind lady who came to my home as planned. She asked a lot of the same health questions that you asked."

"Yes, they like to 'trust and verify.' There have been several times someone has told me one thing and told the 'Paramed' examiner something different. Some customers forget about medications or surgeries from long ago."

"That makes sense because she asked for details around Paula's death with such concern and empathy."

"That's good to hear." Janise smiled empathetically.

"Yes, but the whole meeting went sideways when she asked me to get on the scale."

They both laughed.

"I am pleased that she was able to schedule you so quickly. This now allows for the insurance company to work simultaneously as we work to get everything in order. Plus, once it's done, we can check insurance off of your to-do list."

"All joking aside, I am surprised, Janise. You know that I watched my beautiful sister wither before my eyes, become disabled, and die; and yet I still don't want to think it can or will happen to me."

"I get it, Grace. Your thoughts and feelings are familiar and real." Janise's tone was gentle and reassuring. "Let's take a look at some of the transactions that can take place if you trigger one or several of the events discussed in the Buy-Sell agreement."

"Okay. Give it to me. I'm ready." Grace picked up her pen.

"In the event you become seriously disabled, Joe will have the option to buy your shares over a designated period of time."

"What do you mean by *over a period of time*? Like, how long?" Grace asked.

"Well, when the Buy-Sell agreement is funded with disability buyout insurance, most insurance companies require that you are disabled for at least a year before the buyout clause is activated and the sale of the shares can begin."

"Why does the insurance company have that requirement?" Grace wondered out loud.

"Ideally, as business owners, you will have short-term and long-term disability insurance in place to provide income to you and your family as you recover. But an illness or injury that keeps you from work longer than a year means that you may be out permanently or at least so long that your role in the business may need to be filled. For example, I have seen a couple of people who have been injured in motorcycle accidents. In both cases, it took a year to recover. The difference is that they were continually improving and could see the light at the end of the tunnel. Had they experienced paralysis or injuries that would have prevented their ability to fully recover, they could have triggered a buyout request. In the case of a debilitating disease, you may want to spend that time working on getting better or spend time with your family."

"Okay, that makes sense."

"So, if you find that you have to activate the disability buy-out provision in your contract, you will be paid in installments. In this example, with Joe as the planned successor, he would make payments to you. Then the insurance company would reimburse Joe for the agreed amount. Most insurance companies have three and five-year installment options. Some have a lump-sum option. The lump-sum may cause a sizable tax consequence, so that's why it is essential to include your tax advisor in this conversation."

"Then what happens?" Grace probed.

"Once the disabled business owner is out of the company, it is up to the remaining shareholder(s) as to how the business will move forward. Would Joe want to bring in a business partner or hire someone with your expertise? By using insurance, the company's cash flow is not adversely affected. Most importantly, your relationship with Joe and your family can continue to thrive."

"Well, what happens if I die?" Grace asked, feeling what a strange idea that was to entertain.

"If you die, that will most certainly be a triggering event. In that case, Joe would be buying your shares from your trust or estate. If there were no plans in place, an unintended business partner could determine the fate of the business." Janise said it all so matter-of-factly.

"Who would want to jump in before Joe has a chance to buy and take over the business? I don't know anyone who would do that."

"Oh, you'd be surprised as to who would want to take over this business. It could be a former employee who sees an opportunity to step in and take over or wreak havoc. It could be a competitor or a supplier who sees a chance to increase their market share. It could be a number of people, and since you would no longer be with us, Joe wouldn't have much say in the matter. If the estate chooses to sell to the highest bidder, it could be anyone. However, with the Buy-Sell agreement in place, Joe or your successor will work with your team to follow through with a buy-out. Depending on how the agreement is set up, the life insurance will pay either the company or the shareholders. They will, in turn, use the insurance money to buy the shares from your trust or estate. However, if there is no legal agreement in place, your beneficiaries have no requirement nor obligation to sell their shares back to Joe or the company."

Grace's eyes widened with surprise. "You mean if my family decided they want to take over the business or become partners with Joe, they could do that?"

"Without a legal contract in place, that's correct. That is the purpose of the Buy-Sell Agreement. It is to prevent a 'wild, wild west' scenario. Once the shares are purchased, Joe could continue on with the mission and vision of the company."

"Is it that simple?"

"Well, it is simple in theory, but it may not be easy. If the heirs decide to put up a fight, it can become expensive and messy. They may not prevail, but it's a free country, and some people fight, even if it is out of sheer emotional distress and pain."

"Yeah, I've seen some of that. What if I decide to depart or retire?" Grace asked, feeling more comfortable with this option after her last exercise.

"Let's say that you have a talk with Joe and let him know that you are putting a plan into motion to retire, and you are ready to sell the company. Hopefully, after this process, you will know to start with your strategy five to ten years in advance. Suppose you have done everything to systemize the business and keep it growing and thriving. In that case, you will have a company that is attractive to Joe or another buyer. So, let's say it is Joe or maybe a younger employee who needs to gain experience, knowledge, and a better credit position. Whoever it is, they would benefit from your long-term planning horizon. That's why it is time to talk with your business broker or investment banker. Your broker will do an assessment of the business and determine if it is best for you to move forward with a stock sale or an asset sale."

"What is the difference?" Grace had never heard those terms before.

Janise took a sip of her tea before she answered. "In an asset sale, you are selling the assets of the business, such as inventory, vehicles, property, equipment, and more. Those assets can be moved to a different company. In a stock sale, you are selling the company's shares, and the company will have a new owner. There are tax and liability considerations with these options, and it is essential to know which will work best for you before deciding."

"So, these are customized choices then?" Grace asked.

"Yes, they are. If someone else in your industry decides to pursue an asset sale, it does not mean you should do the same. There are variables that you may know nothing about."

"Where would we look to find a buyer?" Grace's head was beginning to spin a little.

"Your Business Broker or investment banker will help you with this as well. They know how to position your business with the right potential buyers. Suppose no one in your family or business is in the position or interested in buying the business. In that case, the buyer could be someone interested in your business model, a friendly competitor, a private equity firm, a strategic buyer, or even an Employee Stock Option Plan known as an ESOP.

You may have the good fortune of finding a buyer who seems like a fit based on your vision of the future of the employees and the company."

"That would be nice. I had a colleague who sold to a wonderful lady about three years ago. The negotiations took some time, but she convinced them to sell to her and carry the business note. They agreed because they did not want all of the cash at one time. So far, they have had no issues; and of course, they remain hopeful that she continues to grow the business because they do not want to foreclose and take the company back. They are busy enjoying the payment that she sends."

Janise nodded and smiled. "That is a perfect example of what is possible. As you will see with all of the options, there is a degree of risk. In one case, there is not as much risk when the buyer is a cash buyer. In many cases, the cash buyer will typically ask for a discounted price, which could be 20% or more. In that case, you'd undoubtedly want to look at what you need to get out of the deal and how a cash sale would affect your tax position."

"You know the old saying—cash is king! In this case, with the discount and the taxes, I would have to think about what kind of king will I be left with."

"Exactly. Cash is not as simple as it sounds."

"Well, I can see the advantages and disadvantages of cozying up to my friendly competitor, as they know the market and they typically know a lot of our customers; because every once in a while, we hear about them trying to get a foot in the door. In reality, some of our friendly competitors might be the best fit for taking over our business. If we were to negotiate with them, how would we know they won't steal our information?"

"That's a great question. Your broker should be there to vet all serious buyers on your behalf. All serious buyers should be submitting a 'letter of intent' before you disclose your business financials. They must sign a Nondisclosure Agreement, which keeps the business's financial and trade secrets confidential for some time after the sale is completed. You also want to be careful sharing trade secrets with family members and professionals who are not bound by your nondisclosure agreement. It is easy to slip into a conversation and realize that what you are divulging may come back to harm you later."

"So often, I hear of the seller staying in the company once it is sold. Are we required to stay in business to help the new buyer?" Grace asked enthusiastically.

I've been wanting to ask someone this for a while!

"No, that is something that you would negotiate during the escrow process. I have seen deals where the new owners do not want the old owners to continue in the business, so they leave at the close of the sale. Other times, the new owners want the former owners to stay for two years (or more) to ensure a smooth transition of contracts and relationships. I have also seen the selling owners negotiate six-month agreements if they no longer want to be there. In a couple of transactions, I have seen the old owners stay indefinitely as leaders in the business or as working employees. There are so many options, and you would have to look at your circumstances at that time. But I can assure you that in most of these scenarios, a non-compete clause or contract will be a provision."

"How long does it take a business to sell?"

Janise lifted her shoulders for a moment, indicating that it wasn't an easy answer. "If the market is strong and the stars are all aligned, it can take as little as six months. But don't count on it. I had this conversation with my friend Jay, who is a very experienced business broker. He told me it takes anywhere from eighteen months to five years, with two years being the average."

"My goodness, that sounds exhausting!" Grace exclaimed.

Janise nodded. "It could be exhausting for both parties. There is a lot that has to happen. The business has to be valued, and they may need to verify everything from inventory to employees. In some cases, both the buyer and the seller can experience 'deal fatigue.'"

"Deal fatigue?" Grace leaned forward and took a sip of her coffee.

"Yes, that's when one or both sides become frustrated with the negotiations and become irritated and worn down by the entire process. When both sides are not seeing eye to eye, deal fatigue may get the best of them. In some cases, a seller may lose interest in the business and the deal and throw in the towel. You must put in a good faith effort when working with your business broker to avoid a potentially disastrous outcome. Suppose for some reason, communications break down with the buyer, and they want to get as far away as possible from this deal. In that case, they have the right to pay what's called a 'Breakup Fee,' and they will end all negotiations."

"That sounds like business drama!" Grace's stomach was tight at the thought.

"It can be." Janise's eyebrows raised in a way that told Grace this lady had seen some things.

"What are some of the areas of interest or, I guess, points of negotiations that go into the sale of a business?"

"There are so many, and I don't want to overwhelm you. Let's discuss several that are pretty important. A potential buyer will want to know:

How long have you been in business?

Is your business scalable? Does the company have upside potential that may require additional investment, effort, or other risks?

Do you have quality relationships with customers? How diversified is the customer base? Are your best customers in a specific industry or geographic area? Or is there a high customer concentration that may become an issue?

Do you have clarity in the products and services that you offer? What does your pricing look like? What kind of intellectual property do you have? Does your product mix consist of any brand names?

How efficient and productive are your employees? A potential buyer will want to take a look at your employee census: Years of service, age, pay rates vs. market, relatives, skillsets/licensing/certification required, pending retirements, worker's compensation mod rate, unionization, etc.

How up-to-date are your computer and software releases? Is the website being used to increase sales? Are you keeping track of analytics and Search Engine Optimization positioning? Is the point-of-sale system current?

Since every product and service has a cycle and a season, do you have historical records on how your business ebbs and flows?

Where are your competitive threats coming from? Could there be foreign competition such as China or India? Or maybe from the internet, home-based businesses, or franchises? Who are the industry leaders?

What are the details of your facility lease? Are the rates competitive to what the market is currently bearing? What are the terms of the lease? What kind of renewal options do you have? Is the landlord reasonable?

Are all of your required licenses current? Are you aware of the regulatory issues that affect your business?

What are some of the after-sales issues that a new owner needs to be concerned with? Are there any pre-paid services, warranty exposure, returns, employee commitments, equipment leases, and other liabilities to be assumed?

Although you are not a franchisee, those business owners who are franchise business owners will need to address any third-party requirements for a franchisor.

Are there other third-party agreements with dealers, other landlords, Small Business Administration loans, and other entry barriers?

"Wow! We certainly have a lot to work on to get even remotely close to being sales-ready," Grace said while taking copious notes.

"Yes, it is a lot of work. You can see that you can systematically work through a master task list and have your company poised to sell by allowing yourself years instead of months to transition out of the business. This preparation gives you options."

"Oh yes. It makes perfect sense! I can't imagine leaving my team to scramble and pull any of this together for a buyer. Thank you for that education in the sale of a business. What can you tell me about the ESOP? I have heard of ESOPs but know so little about them."

"An ESOP allows employees to become non-voting owners of stock," Janise answered.

"That sounds concerning. I wouldn't want all of the employees to have the leverage to change the way the business functions."

"An ESOP owns the company, and the employees are not running around with possession of the shares. The stock is held in a trust. You, as the owner, would still have control of the company and can sell all or a portion of the company. There are several employee stock option programs being implemented in businesses today. With only 20 to 30% of companies put on the market for sale actually being sold, the ESOP is an option that might work for you, especially if Joe decides that he wants to ride into the sunset close to your targeted retirement date. You would instate a plan that would relieve you of the worry and challenge of finding a future buyer. You will then be able to focus on a smooth exit transition and retirement. This is a conversation you would have with a financial advisor who specializes in this type of transaction. I know exactly the team to help us should you decide to explore this option. It is also important to include a CPA who is also well-versed in the tax consequences of this type of sale."

"How about private equity?" Grace asked.

"Based on your current revenue and business growth, you might catch the interest of a lower-middle market private equity investor. These firms are looking at the scalability and profitability of your business. They are not known for being the warm and fuzzy, sentimental type. So, if you are looking for someone to come in and treat your employees well, you may also find a win-win with a strategic buyer who sees the value of your processes and wants to continue with your team and scale accordingly."

"I am starting to see where all of the advisors and experts come in handy." Grace grinned as she finished her notes for this conversation.

"Yes, with the right team, you can make informed decisions. It is also crucial that you know how to manage your team and team meetings. After all, they are working for *you*."

Something to Think About

"As we discussed, there might be a shortage of potential buyers for the many businesses that currently exist. Have you thought about the challenges that may come with your various certifications if you decided to sell? Or have your son take over?" Janise sat back comfortably.

Grace's eyes widened. "No. I hadn't thought that far in advance. I wanted to make the most of the opportunities in front of me, but wow! I guess that would be an issue considering the business would no longer be a certified woman-owned business. I need to put some thought into what that means in the future. I guess I wouldn't want to secure a lot of relationships that could be lost if the business were no longer woman-owned…"

Oh! Wait a minute! Inspiration had struck.

"Maybe my daughter, who is currently in high school, would like to join her brother in the business in the future?" Grace's mind spun on the possibility. "Yeah, I need to put some thought into that."

"After all, this is a second-generation family business. Maybe my kiddos would want to continue the tradition and add the talents of the third generation. Yeah, that's interesting. I've never thought about this. I'll need at least a week to process this one."

Common Mistakes Made In Business Planning

"Of course. There are so many different things that can go right in putting a business plan together. There's probably even more that can go wrong by neglecting a few things. When isolating all that is to be considered, here are ten areas to contemplate when preparing for the complexities of our business plan:

"**#10 | Not recognizing the need to plan.** You have made it this far, so you already know the only thing I can guarantee is that you will leave this business and will need a plan."

"Oh yes! I'm totally on board with this now! We can check off number ten!" Grace picked up her pen again, ready to take notes on the remaining nine items to keep in mind.

Janise smiled broadly before continuing.

"#9 | The age-old monster, procrastination. I can't tell you how many business owners I speak with who say that if they had another ten or twenty years, they would do things differently—save money, build up the internal leadership, create a succession plan, etc. Don't wait. Take a moment to do what it takes to take care of yourself, but don't take too long. When we procrastinate on implementing an exit strategy, we run the risk of incurring opportunity costs. A missed opportunity could be financially devastating."

"I never procrastinate when I see the importance of action. And now, after realizing how fast time slips by and the impact it can have on a business and family like my sister's, this is the most important plan."

"You have an amazing track record of making things happen, Grace." Janise nodded affirmatively.

"#8 | Waiting until the time when you cannot stand being there one day longer and then insist on selling the business immediately. Truth be told, not everyone is in love with the stress that comes with business or the employees they have hired. Before you get to the point that you're running out of the building with your hair on fire, put together a 'What Would Be Great' list and start there."

"Ha! Hair on fire. Yeah, my new strategy is to leave with style, Janise. I think I am moving in the right direction. Thank you for helping me make that possible."

"It's my pleasure, Grace."

Grace could tell she was soaking in the gratitude.

"**#7 | Not taking into account the effects of the economy on your future growth or decline.** Again, a topic that doesn't require a lot of explanation. In the past two decades, there have been several economic events to remind us of the importance of planning for the worst and expecting the best. There was the Internet stock bubble of 2000 and the tremendous loss during the Great Recession of 2008. After each event, most businesses and the economy managed to find their way back to a position of strength. We don't know what is around the corner nor when the next business crisis will hit. Take your lead for recovery strategies from past life events. Life happens. Things happen. It's not always the most convenient time."

"Yes, it does happen." Grace sighed, thinking about the many losses she and others had suffered because of these events of the last twenty years.

"**#6 | Losing sight of events that can derail your business.** Some people don't realize that they are in an industry that is becoming outdated due to technological advances or shifting in a direction that will no longer make their offerings desirable. Take the pulse of your consumers. And take stock of what is going on in your industry overall. As you analyze the business cycle, determine what your next best move is and make sure to stay abreast of the regulatory requirements and how you can best use technology."

"Noted," Grace said as she finished her notes.

"#5 | Making assumptions that the business value will be based on your passion and intellectual musings. For some, their business is their baby, and nobody wants to hear that they have an ugly baby. And nobody wants to buy an ugly baby. Every business owner must be realistic and make sure their business baby is happy and healthy."

Grace laughed at Janise as she wrote "ugly baby" on her notepad.

"#4 | Making the assumption that key employees will stay forever. Key employees have personal obligations like you. Suppose a key employee suspects instability in their job security. In that case, they become susceptible to what a recruiter is offering to get them to leave you. In that case, they could become your competitor's newest key employees. I know you already take good care of those who take good care of you. Still, you may want to address other ways of instituting an executive benefit plan that encourages your 'rainmakers' to stay with you and not be swayed by outsiders. If you are closer to the sales completion, take a look at those employees who are crucial to the business's stability and negotiate a 'stay bonus' to encourage them to stay for the duration of a transition."

"I'm sure there's a way to incentivize them even more. I'll talk to my team about it."

"#3 | Not having the proper risk management and resources in place to continue the business. We can have the best-laid plan for the business. Still, if we do not have the cash reserves or resources to see that plan through, our business will become another tragic mark in history and close prematurely merely because there are no resources to continue. This situation, of course, affects not only us and our employees but also the suppliers that are counting on us."

"I won't let it happen on my watch," Grace declared.

"I believe you, Grace." Janise's voice was full of respect.

"#2 | Prematurely telling the employees that you are selling or leaving the business.

Your employees may be super close to you and trust you but telling them prematurely that you plan to leave or sell the business may cause them to flee prematurely. Their comprehension and understanding of what it means to sell the business may be fairly different than yours. If there is a mass exodus, their departure can affect the value of the company. Having an exit strategy and a business continuity plan in place could give comfort to your employees if it is appropriately communicated. It may also increase morale and prevent others from jumping ship if there is a loss or departure in the leadership. Think twice before sharing any executive decision that may take place in the distant future."

"Yes, I've learned the hard way that I need to keep very clear boundaries with my employees when it comes to the business's confidential activities," Grace offered.

Janise nodded empathetically. "It's tough to find the line, especially when you care about your employees as much as you do."

"Absolutely."

"#1 | Not putting your experience and expertise in writing. Creating a 'Standard Operating Procedure' is vital to passing on effective practices. A plan that is not in writing is a hobby. The business is a costly hobby and not a viable, fair-market business ready to sell. Without a system in place, a company will not give the buyer comfort that they will receive a return on investment. You've already got a head start on this because of the work you've been doing the last few weeks."

"Yes, I feel pretty good about our system, but that inventory process we did helped me to see the gaps. And we are working to fill them in."

"That's fantastic, Grace. I think you've got these top 10 pretty much figured out. Sure, there are many more opportunities to build a strong foundation. Still, by addressing these, you are well on your way to uncovering other hot issues worth addressing."

"Thanks! Is there anything else I should know about this transition process?"

"Yes, my friend Jay was telling me that one of the main reasons they see business transitions fail is because the business owner cannot let go. There was a story I heard about a family business in which the 85-year-old CEO of a company refused to share his business secrets with his competent daughter and heir apparent, who also worked as an executive in the business. In fact, she sat in the office right next door to his. He refused to let her 'take over his position.' But at 85 years old, what did he think would happen next? What did he think would happen to the business? What would happen to his loyal employees who were blindly counting on him to do the right thing? My biggest question was: Is this behavior expressing an issue of control or the desire to feel needed? My other thought was that he must have had a lack of confidence in those around him. By not sharing his years of experience and the wisdom in his head, this gentleman was inadvertently leading his sheep to the slaughter. If his daughter could not figure out how to pull together the missing pieces on time, the business's value would decline and ultimately fail. All of the equity and her years of service would be lost."

"It is absolutely amazing that this older gentleman would not recognize the fate of his empire. I am so fortunate that my dad did not hoard information. Now, I am not going to say that he had everything in writing and told me everything I needed to know. But I can say I was introduced to all of our customers, and I was always welcome to walk into his office and sit with him during meetings. Those were my early-stage learning sessions. I guess I'd better count my blessings." Grace's eyes filled with gratitude as the memories flooded her mind.

"Oh yes. Based on what I have heard you say, you were in a great position to jump into the driver's seat and keep the business moving forward. Any guesses about what I would like you to work on before our next meeting?"

"Yes, all of those questions about scalability, customers, and business clarity stuff."

"Perfect! Take some time to think about each of the questions, and let's get together in a month to talk about your thoughts and findings."

Prepare to Leave In Style at:
www.LeavingInStyle.com/Resources

Chapter Six

ACCESSORIZE WITH A
DYNAMIC TEAM OF EXPERTS

"GOOD MORNING, JANISE!" Grace greeted her when she saw her face on the computer.

"Hi, Grace. How are you today?" Janise settled into her chair.

"I'm well. You?" Grace asked, noticing that she looked even brighter than usual today. Maybe it was the rich and delicately-printed sapphire blue blouse or the upswept hair. It was hard to tell.

"I'm good. I was so pleased to see the progress you made towards adding clarity to your business goals. After taking your long-term vision and goals and reverse-engineering them into immediate and intermediate actions items, I am confident that you will find the long-term progress to be realistic and attainable."

"I agree, Janise. At first, I was a bit intimidated by the process and concerned that there was no reasonable way to reach such audacious goals. We wrote them down, walked away from them, and then came back to address them one by one. As we determined all of the desired steps, we began taking immediate action and only focusing on what was in front of us. That process made us feel successful every week as we chipped away at our ultimate goal of tremendous growth and scalability."

"Do you think this system will work in other areas within the business?"

"Yes, most definitely. We have created an internal team to go through our company processes, revisit their purpose, and make sure that we are all in alignment. I love this clarity and team approach."

"This is so good to hear. In fact, I thought of you last night as we had a fun little basketball championship party and invited two friends who are die-hard sports fans. I'm always amazed when I watch seasoned athletes work together to create magic on a court, and I realized it was a perfect time to be thinking about that because today, we're going to discuss your team of business advisors.

When I think of the advisors that need to come in and help in your business, I often like to imagine gathering or leveraging a dream team!"

Grace smiled at her bubbly expression.

"I mean, after all, when referring back to our style analogy, working from head to toe, you have the knowledge and the overall leadership vision or personal style. Plus, you have mastered confidence and composure. The business suit is tailored and now let's add the accessories."

"Accessories? That seems like such a minor addition to such a big picture," Grace mused.

"Think about how finished a look is when the smallest of details are considered. When you have quality accessories, they tell a story of preparation and fine-tuning. They add a little extra polish and even pizzazz." Janise's love of fashion made her glow.

"I get it! I can see that, especially because I know that's true with our packaging, too. We have made a name for ourselves in the industry because our prospects and customers know that it is the smallest of details that make their products a cut above. The details and final touches definitely set us apart. So, what small things can we add to this plan to make such a big impression?" Grace was ready.

"You may recall, in our previous meeting, we talked about some of the business contracts that are required and, of course, the expert help you are going to need to make all of that happen."

"Yes, and there was quite a bit. It looks like it's going to get rather expensive. Are those the accessories you are referring to?" Her brow furrowed with a bit of concern.

"Yes, those are certainly some of the accessories."

"We have talked about a variety of accessories, I mean experts, and that seems to be an expensive endeavor. Can't we use one of those online legal companies to get most of the contracts done? When I go to the office supply store, I've also noticed they have some standardized business forms that may be useful as well. What are your thoughts about these resources?"

"That's a common question, Grace, and the best answer I can give is another question: What is it about your business that you feel is standard?" She paused for a moment.

Good question, Grace thought.

"It has been my experience that most businesses are unique enough that the contracts and agreements that pertain to the business should reflect its uniqueness. Since your business documents are also potentially legal documents, if you were to go into a court of law, wouldn't you want an expert to come alongside—one who can explain the processes and procedures put into place? And it's important to note that most attorneys will not support a document they did not create."

"Thank you. That's a perspective I had not contemplated. Okay, so we'll go the expensive-but-wise route. Can you tell me a little bit about the various experts I need to be looking for?" Grace had her pen poised above her notebook.

"I'd be happy to, but expensive is relative. Paying for an expert's time up front may save you much more in the long run. I'd like to give you some preliminary information about what you should ponder when selecting the perfect accessories. In fact, you may have some of these professionals already working with you and your business. Do you currently have an Accountant, Accounting Consultant, or a Certified Public Accountant (CPA) working with you?"

"We work with two of the three. Should we have an accountant who works outside of our business as well?"

"Good observation. No, the title Accountant and Accounting Consultant are the same professional. Each state's regulations vary as to which title the accountant can use if they are not a Certified Public Accountant. Here in California, one who has an accounting degree can present themselves to the public as an Accounting Consultant and not as an Accountant. This has nothing to do with your in-house accounting personnel."

"That is a bit confusing." Grace's eyebrows raised as she worked to understand the differences.

"Yes, it most certainly can be confusing, especially if you are working in multiple states. We will talk about these professionals a bit more in a moment," Janise assured.

"To answer your question, yes, I do work with a CPA. And for the past ten years, I have worked with Deanna, our Accounting Consultant."

"Great, can you tell me how Deanna works with you and your business?" Janise picked up her pen, clearly ready to take notes.

"Sure! Deanna comes out and meets with us every month to make sure that we are meeting our financial benchmarks. She has been instrumental in helping us understand our profit and loss and how they affect our balance sheet and bottom line. For example, at one point, we were experiencing a cycle of tremendous growth. Our profits appeared to double in less than a year. When we began implementing a strategy of expanding the business into a new area, Deanna looked at our financials. She helped us realize that expanding too quickly could derail our profits and endanger our core market. She helped us understand that if we were to expand into a new market, we would need to take into account the salaries and benefits associated with hiring more employees and the equipment needed to support that growth."

"It sounds like Deanna clearly understands your business. Does she also file your corporate taxes and complete corporate audits?"

"No, she helps us by compiling all of the documentation needed for Rick, our CPA. He processes our taxes and reviews our statements when warranted. I would say Deanna's role falls right between our bookkeeper and our CPA. She is more like our outsourced CFO."

"Okay, then let me share a little bit more detail as to what a CPA can do."

Grace leaned forward to listen.

Accountants, Accounting Consultants, and Certified Public Accountants (CPA)

"An accountant will help with a wide range of financial issues that may come up. They will address the financial issues, accounting issues, compliance with tax (payroll multistate tax compliance), Internal Revenue Service (IRS) audit issues, and sometimes business valuations. They also review your accounts receivables and accounts payables—your liabilities and your inventories. Someone with this expertise will recognize what should and should not be reflected on the balance sheet to boost the business's value. For example, you may have personal/business use items such as car payments that are adversely affecting the business's cash flow projections. Your CPA can also do what your accountant does. Still, they are uniquely licensed to prepare certified audited financial statements and, if necessary, provide representation with the IRS."

"That sounds scary! Whenever I hear the word IRS, I shudder!" Grace half-laughed.

"Oh yes, I hear that quite often. That's why it's so nice to have an accounting professional that works with you on a strategic basis as opposed to a forensic basis."

A what? Grace's forehead scrunched in confusion.

"Let me put that another way. When do you meet with your CPA?" Janise asked.

"In February, after our books have closed for the previous year."

"And what does that process look like?" She was taking careful notes.

"Once our books are closed out, I schedule an appointment and then go meet with our CPA and have our taxes done."

"Is that the first time you are talking to your CPA about what took place in your business during the prior year?" Janise probed.

"In most cases, yes," Grace answered.

Should I be talking to my CPA more?

"Well, let's see. Are you surprised at the amount you have to pay in taxes each year?"

Grace scrunched her nose at the mention of taxes and surprise. "Yes, it is like waiting for a shoe to drop. I hate that part. I sit nervously with the checkbook on the desk and my pen in hand, waiting to hear what I owe for the previous year!"

"I can only imagine. What would be different if you had a tax strategy all year long that included several ways to take advantage of the tax codes written to help business owners?" Janise offered a new possibility.

"Wow, I have never thought about that. I think I would feel more focused and calmer knowing that I would not have the stress of wondering what I owed each year. Actually, the concept makes me feel more relaxed right now." Grace shook her head as she remembered last year's taxes.

Ugh, it would have been nice to see that coming!

"Well, that is the difference between working with an accountant that is a forensic collector of old information and a strategic planner who helps you create a strategy to maximize your tax advantages."

"I'll take one of the latter, please. That sounds amazing! We should explore what it would look like to have someone who is willing to work with us from the beginning of the year. That would be a lot less stressful. To be honest, I can recall Deanna offering to assist us this way, and I never took the time to follow up. I am definitely going to do that now."

"That's a great idea! So, it's also good to know that some CPAs will do a business valuation. In contrast, others prefer to refer that to a business broker or business valuation company. I will share more about those professionals in a moment. But first, let's discuss attorneys."

"Oh boy!" Grace smiled. "I hope you know how to find a good one!"

Attorney

"Do you currently have an attorney working with you in your business?"

"Do you mean on staff or on retainer?" Grace asked.

"Great question, I meant on retainer. Based on the size of your business, I figured there was a pretty good chance you would not have one on staff."

"No. We have been quite fortunate and have not had many legal issues. Dad had a friend who was an attorney. He helped Joe and me draft the terms of our business relationship, but he has long since retired." Grace sat back in her chair.

"Ah yes, family friend attorneys are so good to know. Since he's retired, let's talk about what you need to investigate when looking for an attorney to help you with your business contracts. Several niche-focused legal professionals can assist you as you plan the legacy of your business, one of which is an estate planning attorney."

"Oh, we have been working with an estate planning attorney to resolve some of Paula's estate issues, and I've been delighted with her help. How can an estate planning attorney help us in our business?"

"More and more estate planning attorneys are specializing in business law as well, so you may find that an estate planning attorney also has a specialty in business law. Suppose you are working with a law firm. In that case, the estate planning and business planning attorneys may work together because, ultimately, as you have witnessed, the business can definitely affect the outcome of your estate."

"That's interesting and so true. I have never put much thought into how all of that is intertwined."

You'd think I'd have realized that after the year I just survived!

"Yes, I speak with a lot of business owners who inform me that the shares of their business are being held in their family's revocable living trust. For the purpose of business, we want to make sure that you have an attorney that is familiar with writing Buy-Sell agreements."

"If you have any referrals, I'd be happy to get a list of trusted attorneys from you." Grace always got along better with trusted referrals.

"Absolutely. I am networked with some incredible professionals and will share my list with you. For now, let's talk about the next type of advisor you'll need on your team: the banker."

Bankers

"What type of relationship do you have with your bank and your banker?"

"I have a good working relationship with my banker. We talk on an as-needed basis, but when I have questions about our lines of credit or any type of issues that arise with inventory, Dabora is always responsive." Grace was obviously grateful for her team and their responsiveness.

"That's good to hear because the banking relationship may be one of the most untapped relationships that a business owner has. Bankers can also provide assistance with strategic planning for the future of your business. By including your banker in your meetings, you can access clarity and updates on outstanding and available commercial loans, lines of credit, and even solutions to help with your employees. Some of them include payroll, too."

"Wow, I never thought of inviting my banker in to help me with my business planning strategies. But it makes perfect sense!"

Why haven't I thought of this?

"All these little things that never occur to us while we're building a business." Janise smiled. "Ready to talk about appraisers?"

"Sure!"

Business Appraisers

"The last time we met, you mentioned that your dad had the business valued before completing his estate planning. What do you remember about the process?" Janise asked.

"Wow, that was so long ago." Grace leaned further back in her chair and stared at one of the last family photos with her dad hanging on the other side of her office while her mind searched for the details. "I remember very little about that process. I was so young and so busy working in the business. I can't say that I recall anything that was going on." Suddenly, a memory emerged. "Wait, I do remember Dad working closely to ensure that the inventory numbers were accurate as well as the other accounts payable and receivable parts of the business. As I got older, I attended as many of his meetings as I did when I was a young girl. Those meetings started to make a little more sense. However, I still did not understand the magnitude of what was happening as Dad and three or four men brainstormed how to build value in the business."

"That makes sense. Those men were most likely your dad's advisors, or in our language, they were your dad's accessories. I want to share a little more about some of the different professionals. They can help by providing a business appraisal. Do you understand why it is important to have a business valuation?" Janise questioned gently.

"Yes, but I can't say that I fully understand why it would be something that we need to do regularly."

"This is a great question for you to address with your CPA. Although you may not need a formal business appraisal done regularly, it may become important as you approach a change of ownership or retirement or even business succession." Janise sat forward and rested her elbows on her desk.

"Is my CPA the only person that I can talk to about this type of planning?" Grace asked.

Janise shook her head. "No, some investment bankers, business brokers, commercial real estate brokers, and even some insurance companies will create a preliminary or simplified business valuation. Certain business transactions will require a qualified appraisal, which is more comprehensive and must be completed by a certified valuation professional. Suppose you engage a company that specializes in business valuations. In that case, the evaluation professional is typically coming from within the accounting field and has advanced credentials such as a Certified Financial Analyst or a Certified Public Accountant. Both experts will analyze the company's strengths and weaknesses, price, and earnings in comparison to the industry averages. They look at your tangible assets and your intangible assets. Those include your copyrights, patents, customer lists, management team, manufacturing and distribution processes, and any types of agreements you have in place. The assets of your business are also quite important."

Business Broker
(or Mergers & Acquisition Professional)

"I have a friend who is a business broker. I have also heard others talk about selling their business using a Mergers & Acquisition team. Can you explain to me the difference between a business broker and mergers and acquisitions professional?" Grace asked, grateful for this opportunity to ask all of the questions she never felt comfortable asking.

"Absolutely. These professionals locate buyers and help to sell businesses. They can be extremely helpful in your business's presale preparation, helping you make sure that you have a nice internet presence such as a website that potential buyers can go to. They also may help you position the business so that it is attractive to buyers. When I asked my friend, Jay, who is a business broker and nonpracticing CPA, this same question, he explained it this way: There are two different markets for buying and selling of businesses. The rule of thumb is that business brokers work in the middle market, which are businesses being sold from $2 to $10 million dollars. The Mergers and Acquisitions market are those businesses being sold from $10 million to $50 billion and beyond."

"That was quite helpful, thank you. I've always wanted to know that." Grace hoped her appreciation showed through her expression.

"A little clarity goes a long way. Some business brokers work in the small 'mom-and-pop' market. That includes businesses with revenues of less than $2,000,000. Now, let's talk about financial advisors and wealth managers."

Financial Advisor / Wealth Manager

"Another key professional who should be involved in the eventual sale and your future departure in the business is your wealth manager."

Janise must think that I am a mogul.

"A wealth manager? Isn't that only for people like the Gettys, the Rockefellers, and the Kennedys? I have a financial advisor, but do I need a wealth manager as well?" Grace asked sincerely.

"Well, sometimes they're one and the same. I prefer to use the term wealth manager because a financial advisor can be such a broad term. Most people don't realize it, but your lender is also a financial advisor, even though they do not necessarily work in the capacity of advising you on how to invest your money. Why don't you tell me a little bit about your financial advisor?"

"I met my financial advisor, Carl, at one of those lovely dinner meetings where we learned retirement basics. He was kind and helpful and recommended that I do a couple of things to help set aside money for retirement."

"That's great! Has he ever asked about your business and the future value of your business and what it means to your retirement plan?" Janise probed.

"No. He did ask some preliminary questions and then put them all into software that made a nice presentation. We really didn't go over much about what's going on in the business." Grace paused, thinking about their interactions. "Actually, when Carl and I get together, he loves to tell me about his vintage car collection."

"It sounds like Carl may be more comfortable working with families and more simplified solutions."

"Shouldn't he be doing more for business owners?" Grace said, feeling a bit of anger surge.

"No, I wouldn't say that. Carl might be quite bright. Let's look at it this way. Who is your ideal customer?"

"Well, I prefer working with luxury brands and high-end cosmetic companies," Grace answered quickly.

"And with that in mind, is it of interest to you to pursue business in the corrugated box market?" she coaxed.

"Not. At. All. That is not of interest to me at all. In fact, when I go to business conferences, I attend the workshops that keep me on top of innovation in the luxury markets only."

"Exactly. So, let's take that same scenario and apply it to Carl. There is simply too much to know in the financial and investment space. Those advisors who know a little about many different things are typically generalists and may refer to their more advanced colleagues when the need arises. You should be cautious of the person who is an all-knowing one-stop-shop. Wouldn't you be a little suspicious if someone told you they were a neurologist, a cardiologist, and a general practitioner?

Grace chuckled at how simple that analogy made it. "Dad had a friend like that. He called him 'Mr. Know It All.' He was always pursuing my dad for business, but Dad wanted no part of his friend's advice."

"Yes, I see that you get the picture. The advisor who chooses to work with business owners recognizes that advanced training may be necessary to focus on that particular niche. If the business sector is not of interest to Carl, that's fine. There are plenty of wealth managers who find it quite exciting and specialize in working solely with business owners. Those professionals are actually comfortable working with the analysis and multifaceted complexities that come with the business. It is simply not for everyone."

"That makes a lot of sense. You sure have a way of making all of this a little simpler."

"Thank you. That is my goal!" Janise smiled widely before continuing. "Allow me to share a story to illustrate the importance of a wealth manager. There was a couple in their early fifties who worked in a business they started thirty years ago. They grew the company from $3,000 to $5,000,000 during that time. Most of the growth from their hard work has come during the second half of their time in business. They decided they wanted to retire young, host dinner parties, and travel extensively. They could also see the market softening a little and thought they should sell the business while they could. They worked feverishly to prepare the business, so it would sell at or above their desired price. Offers were coming in within the $8 to $10 million range. They were pleased because it appeared to be all they needed to live comfortably, maintain their current lifestyle, and vacation a lot. The business broker reviewed the offers with the couple. Still, before he would respond to any offer, he insisted that they speak with their wealth manager to fully understand what was going to happen with the net proceeds of the sale."

Grace leaned forward to grab her cup of coffee while Janise continued with the story.

"So, the couple, although a little annoyed, contacted their wealth manager and brought her up to date with what they were doing. They were quite confident that the numbers they had run would serve them well. They shared particulars of the sale and the vision of their future together. When their wealth manager reviewed all of the information, she shared a breakdown of how long the projected net proceeds would last based on their current lifestyle, life expectancy, and future vision. They were so alarmed to see that their money would run out in less than twenty years. This couple was mortified. They thought that they were going to live happily ever after. Still, the reality was that they hadn't thought about some key challenges, such as the potential for increased health issues, living too long, tax consequences, and a manageable budget."

Grace gulped her drink. *Wow, that's a pretty significant discrepancy!*

"Fortunately, it wasn't too late to take the business off the market and stop the sale. They weren't too old nor too tired to continue growing the business and their savings. In fact, with the wealth manager's help, they could put some financial strategies in place, so when they made the next attempt, they would come out winners. One recommendation was for them to do some research and determine which states they would be willing to live in, as permanent residents before attempting to sell the business again."

"Wow, when we hear about receiving a lump sum of millions, we assume that it truly will last forever. But who thinks about living to 100 years old? Good catch, wealth advisor," Grace mused.

"Exactly. That's why it is so essential to engage a wealth manager in your business's exit process because they will show you how those dollars will work for you over time. The idea is to secure the golden goose and live off of the eggs. Still, if you don't have a proper plan, you may find yourself looking for a job in a decade when you realize the money is running out."

"That is a scary thought." Grace shook her head.

"Exactly. And what if your body is too tired to get up and go to work? This is the retirement fear that is greater than dying—outliving your money."

"Oh, my goodness! I would be mortified at the thought of having to go back to work at seventy-five or eighty years old. Living with my daughter or son after all of those years of independence would be unbearable.

That is certainly not something that I want in my future! What should I be looking for in a wealth manager?"

"Well, financial advisors and wealth managers work under a lot of different titles, certifications, and designations. I would suggest asking some of your business colleagues as well as interviewing advisors. You will see some with designations such as Chartered Financial Consultant, Certified Financial Planner, Certified Retirement Planner, Registered Investment Advisor, and more. Be sure that you are working with someone who is a fiduciary and puts *your* best interest first. As always, I am happy to share my connections and resources with you."

"Thank you. I am certainly gonna need guidance in this area," Grace said.

"It's my pleasure. Now, let's talk about insurance."

Grace set her teacup down and nodded for Janise to go on.

Life Insurance Professional

"Let me guess, is Carl your life insurance professional?" Janise didn't try to hide her smirk.

"Yes," Grace laughed. "How did you know?"

Janise's smile widened. "Because sometimes wealth managers and financial advisors also address life insurance needs. Keep in mind that is not always the case because some fiduciaries are not allowed to offer life insurance. It's a long and complicated story for another day. The point is, this is another area of expertise where life insurance professionals prefer to solely work with other financial advisors while focusing on risk management and insurance solutions."

"If I recall correctly, I remember reading this in your bio when you spoke at our conference a few months ago. You started in retirement planning and moved into an area of working with business owners, right?" Grace asked.

"That is correct. When I started in this industry over twenty-five years ago, I worked at a major insurance company. I learned a lot about the insurance industry. I had to pass several securities exams to process trades and assist insurance and financial advisors. After several years, I began working with the public and designing retirement plans for employees. There were so many times when I was sitting and talking with employees, knowing that if I managed that 401k plan and the owner dies and/or the business fails, all of our work would not benefit everyone as hoped. That's why I decided to switch gears and create more impact for everyone."

"That makes perfect sense, Janise. Thank you for making that shift. Heaven knows all of my employees and I need you to ensure that all this work does not turn out to be in vain. We all need this business to flow into new ownership as gracefully, no pun intended, as possible."

"A life insurance professional will work closely with your team to make sure that all of your desired plans are properly funded in the event of a death or disability. By taking these risks off the table, this will allow you to maximize your income potential for your wealth preservation and care for those who are important to you."

"This all sounds like an intricate dance," Grace ruminated out loud.

"It is." Janise paused. "You could also look at it this way. When you see a team of attorneys walking into court, they don't all know the same thing. They all happen to be attorneys and have specialties in different areas. They all come together for the greater good of the customer."

"That is a perfect visual analogy! I love it!"

"An insurance professional who understands the proper structure of the policies and knows how to seek out the insurance companies will recognize the nuances of business and cater to the needs of business owners." Janise stopped to take a sip of water. "You ready for the next team member?"

Business Consultant

"There are a variety of specialties with accountants, attorneys, and financial advisors. There are also a lot of ways that you can go when it comes to leveraging business consultants."

"Are business consultants and business coaches the same thing? Who is who?" Grace had been trying to figure this one out for a while.

"You are full of great questions, Grace. Some business consultants call themselves business coaches and vice versa. In business, however, consultants tend to be experts in a particular field or subject matter. A business consultant will help with your business's day-to-day continuity planning and support you as you structure

172 | Leaving In Style

and shape a company that will meet your long-term goals. For example, if you needed to streamline the shipping methods in your warehouse, you would have a consultant who has an expertise in logistics visit you on-site, review, and analyze your current practices. Then, they would come back and make recommendations on warehouse configurations and processes that will streamline your logistics, right?"

"That's right."

"Now, coaches tend to be excellent communicators who will ask questions based on the information supplied by you or your team. Those poignant questions will help you come to a conclusion or strategy that works best for the business. They typically do not go out and do analysis and advise you on what to do."

"That would be similar to having a business development ally sitting on my side of the table?" Grace asked.

"You can certainly look at it that way. It may be beneficial to have a business consultant attend your annual meetings to better understand the big picture and long-term strategy. They can also ask questions that you may not have thought about and help you grow your business. They are helpful for business owners like you who don't operate in a franchise model, where you would have a franchise developer who is fully aware of your desired outcome to go to when you have questions."

"Yes, I guess I have worked with both consultants and coaches over time and lots of the other professionals. I never thought of getting them all together in the same room. It's a bit intimidating, to be honest." Grace felt the anxiety that always invaded her chest when she was about to try something new.

"Well, hopefully, knowing more about who does what has taken away some of that intimidation. It's worth the discomfort to have multiple and varied perspectives and expertise working to make your business profitable and ready for you to leave in style when it's time."

"I can definitely see that. It looks like I already have several of these *accessories* on my team and need a few more to finish *the outfit.* I am guessing that my homework for the month is to take a look at your list of resources and start to shop for those finishing touches?"

"Yes, ma'am," Janise responded.

"Oh, and before we go. During our last conversation, you were tossing around the idea of your son and daughter continuing the family business. Have you come to any conclusions?"

"Yes, thanks for reminding me. I spoke with my kids, and as much as I would like to see them continue the legacy, they have absolutely no interest in 'working this hard'—their words, not mine." Grace smiled and shrugged her shoulders before she continued. "Although Joe and I are close in age, he is still interested in entertaining a purchase in the future."

"Good deal. Then we will continue on the path as planned. Are you ready?"

"I think so. With you guiding me, we can create a road map and a plan that provides peace of mind for everyone who is intimately involved with this business. You will be here to help as we build our infrastructure, right?"

"Absolutely. We will work as a team to get everything in order. I am happy to serve as a facilitator when coordinating the accessories and working with a team of experts." She grinned widely. "So, let's recap. We have already talked about the past experiences and challenges in the business. We are currently addressing the areas of improvement and proper documentation. We have outlined what the future will look like when the predetermined key performance indicators have been met. I'd say we are ready to continue to work down the list and check the boxes. Once we have the succession plan in place, the work in and on the business will be continuous to ensure that the business stays on target all the way to the transition."

"Will we meet again soon?" Grace asked.

"Yes, I am here for the long haul. As you know, the conference is fast approaching. I am looking forward to seeing you in person again at the Boca Raton Resort and Club."

"Me too! I think… No, I know that my business and my head are in a much better place than they were when we initially met. I can't wait to sit, have dinner and wine, and reflect on all of our hard work."

I can almost taste the famous key lime tarts that I am going to enjoy as I sit across the table from this lady in one of my favorite places.

"It's your hard work, Grace. You are doing and have done all of the heavy lifting, and I am so proud of you for being so inquisitive and exploring what is possible."

"Janise, you have made this process so safe, interesting, and more palatable (and fashionable) than I could have ever imagined. I've got you on the calendar and look forward to chatting and seeing you at the conference in a few months."

Prepare to Leave In Style at:
www.LeavingInStyle.com/Resources

Chapter Seven

REFLECT AND REFINE
WITH ANNUAL REVIEWS

GRACE SAT DOWN in the dark leather chair where this business relationship began. She set her purse down and looked into the face of the person who had helped her get her business ready for her to leave in style. They had worked together virtually over the past year and were meeting in person once again at the annual conference where they had first connected.

"It is so great, Janise, that we were able to come back here to this beautiful Boca Raton Resort. There is so much that we have to get caught up on. I don't know where to begin!"

"Let's start with it's so good to see you in person!" Her enthusiasm was genuine.

"Oh, my goodness, Janise, we have survived! This past year has been surreal. When we talked about preparing for uncertainty, we could have never imagined in our wildest dreams, or should I say nightmares, that we would be forced to shut down as a country and a world due to a pandemic. It sounds like something straight out of a science fiction movie. I can recall us discussing the events and fall-out after the internet bust earlier in the millennium and then the housing crisis that crippled the economy. Did you ever think we would be hit by a global pandemic?" Grace's eyes were wide with the feeling of shock she still felt about the nightmare that had ensued.

"I can't say I saw that one coming. You know that I preach the mantra, 'plan for the worst and expect the best;' but I must admit, that turn of events was quite the ride."

"Although our meetings were virtual, I knew you were experiencing a lot of challenges. I think you did a wonderful job, and I am curious to know how do *you* think you did."

"At first, it was tough, like sleepless nights kind of tough. We were stunned with disbelief like so many of our friends and began working towards stabilizing and surviving the tsunami of uncertainty. Since we had already started working on a business continuity plan, we simply took those tools and made them work for us. The first thing we did was adhere to the mandates as they were announced by the governor. That meant that we closed the business immediately to our customers or any outside suppliers. Most of our office staff shifted quickly and worked from home. We did not want to furlough our employees, so we spread out the work so there could be three lighter shifts working in the warehouse."

Grace took a sip of her ice-cold Berry Fizz.

"Eventually, our business even picked up because there were so many people at home shopping online. Our customers had more orders than usual coming through their websites and third-party suppliers. After all, almost everything shipped comes in a big box. And within those big boxes are our little boxes."

"I'm so glad that your business was one of those that was still needed during these times."

"Me too, but it wasn't easy. Our team held countless virtual meetings as we followed the protocols that we had begun to document. What impeccable timing. Had this pandemic taken place a year earlier, we would not have known where to begin, nor would we have a map to point us in the right direction." Grace smiled gratefully at Janise and took another sip. "I found our virtual calls to be an escape, and I internally compartmentalized what was going on around me and focused on the business at hand and what was on the meeting agenda. A lot of what I learned from you helped me prepare for my first all-inclusive annual corporate meeting. Thank you for attending that, by the way! I think it was good, even though we had to conduct it virtually." Grace shook her head as she remembered. "I have been holding video meetings for years, and from time to time, I would get pushback from prospective customers. Now, everyone is an expert. They are thriving from this form of communication because at least we can see one another, and they don't have to hold the phone to their ear for an hour! I guess I can say that some good has come from the tragic event."

"Well," Janise started, smiling, and grabbing her tall glass of mango iced tea. "I enjoyed being a part of your virtual annual meeting a few days ago and am proud of your progress. The timing of the meeting was perfect since we already planned to connect in person today. From your vantage point, tell me, how do you think the annual meeting went?" She sat back and took a long sip.

"It was great! It was so different! This is the first time I felt we had a productive meeting and that I actually understood what was going on the entire time."

"That sounds great! So, different than the others?" Janise probed for more details.

"Well, using the sample agenda that's provided on your website was a good start. It was so easy for our team to personalize it to reflect what I wanted to discuss. In the past, if we had questions regarding our insurance coverages or legal or financial questions, we made a note. We then had to call to ask our advisors those questions and then bring them to another meeting. This time, I contacted all of our advisors well in advance and requested their attendance at the meeting. I provided them with the agenda and questions that I needed them to address during our annual meeting. I felt so empowered and in control of my own process."

I don't know how it never occurred to me to do this before!

"When you contacted your advisors to request their attendance at your annual meeting, how did they respond?" Janise asked.

"They were surprised that I asked and were quite agreeable. We planned far enough in advance and not too close to tax season so that everyone could be present." Grace took another sip of her favorite drink.

"Do you feel that having them all present saved time and money?"

"Absolutely! I can't tell you how much we've spent on billable hours in the past, going back and forth with questions and misunderstandings that could have been addressed all at one time. As you know, some of my advisors are compensated differently, and some do not charge to attend our meetings. However, our CPA and attorney do charge billable hours, so we paid for ninety minutes of their time."

"How did you decide to buy ninety minutes of their time and not one hour or two hours?" Janise sunk more deeply into the comfy lounge chair.

"Well, we did not want to waste time and money, so we created an especially tight agenda and made sure that we discussed all of the business items that we wanted their input on during that time frame."

"So, you did not want them to present their reports and leave?"

"No, we felt that it was important that they listened to the information being provided by the other advisors in case they had questions or additional input. And they all listened with great interest."

"Now that you have conducted your first meeting with the new format, what worked best? What did you like about the meeting?" Janise took another sip of her refreshing beverage.

"Certainly, I like that we opened the meeting with a reflection on our strategy for last year. My key staff worked very hard to provide updates on the areas they manage. Before this meeting, they never felt so involved in the success of the meeting. Then we put all of our energy into preparing a strategy for the business's growth and structure. Joe took the lead on discussing the progress we've made creating structure and a succession plan that was not for us as leaders. By Joe taking it a step further and creating a structure for the entire company, everyone could see where they fit in the quest for success. He did a wonderful job illustrating a succession plan for every leader in every department, don't you think?"

"Yes, it was quite productive, and I could see the impact on your employees' faces. They did enjoy owning part of the success. How did it make you feel?"

"I felt calm and relieved. I feel that my business has a future and will not go away as Paula's did. My employees now have a purpose and know exactly what to do in the event of an emergency. Having that plan has done wonders to boost morale. We've had more employees come up with greater ideas now than ever." Grace beamed as she thought about some of those brilliant ideas and how they were already up-leveling the company.

"That was an excellent by-product to putting a succession plan in place," Janise affirmed.

"Yes, it was. I did not expect Joe to get excited and offer more input. I think it made him feel like we are that one pretty amazing team." Grace paused, obviously overwhelmed with gratitude, while she thought about what else she enjoyed about the meeting. "I can't believe I am going to say this, but I actually enjoyed delving deeper into the financial statements. As we reviewed our corporate records, discussed our tax returns, the profit and loss statements, accounts receivable issues, and so much more, I truly felt as strong and confident as I did when I wore my first 'power suit' many years ago. The nice thing is that we have finally listened to Deanna and have engaged her to do more as our outsourced CFO consultant. She has taught us how to be more forward thinking. We couldn't be happier. Her financial report card is perfect for explaining where we are financially."

"Yes, I was impressed with her work," agreed Janise.

"Our new CPA also understands the importance of pre-planning and is a vital part of our comprehensive approach to a win-win tax strategy. We now have quarterly meetings on the calendar for the remainder of the year, so we will no longer have surprises at year-end. No more forensic tax shockers for us." Grace breathed a big sigh of relief. "The financial advisor discussed our employees' 401k plan and some suggestions on how to improve it. Both our financial advisor and our CPA talked with us about creating an executive retirement plan so that we can stop contributing to the 401k plan. We can also stop worrying about those huge penalties that are levied when the executives save more into the retirement plan than the employees."

"Oh, they want you to pass the 'nondiscrimination testing' of your employee's retirement plan," Janise interjected.

"Yes, that was the phrase they used: 'nondiscrimination testing.' I had no idea at all what the term meant. I now know it is a test to make sure the 401k retirement plan is not favoring the executives or highly compensated employees over the other employees. They were able to clear things up rather quickly."

"In the past, would your advisors ask similar questions that needed to be relayed to another professional?" Janise asked.

186 | Leaving In Style

"Yes, and I would have to relay the question even though I did not fully understand what I was asking. It was kind of like 'the telephone game' we played as kids. I was never sure if I relayed the full and accurate question, and I had to attempt to give 'correct' answers to my accountant." Grace rolled her eyes to emphasize her belief in her ability to do that well.

"What a great use of time to incorporate all of these priority subjects into one meeting!"

"Yes, it was." Grace nodded enthusiastically.

"Are there any other moments that stand out?" Janise looked thrilled about the progress.

"When we discussed the value of the business and celebrated how much growth we've seen in the past year. During the business valuation presentation, I was happy to hear you recommend to our corporate attorney that he increase our business value documented in our Buy-Sell agreement to align with the assessment that came from the finalized business valuation. That became the benchmark for our future growth and negotiations. The life and disability insurances we put in place can potentially benefit both the company and my children. My kids are watching my nephew and his dad struggle since Paula's passing. All of our hearts are aching for them, and I don't want my children to have that kind of experience. I want them to be productive citizens, and I also want them to have the means to continue on the path and dreams we have spent long hours talking about. Just because I am gone does not mean everyone's world should fall apart. I think it is enough to lose a parent—why do you have to lose home stability and planned college opportunities as well? The amount of life insurance you recommended was reasonable and appropriate."

"You have put a lot of thought into this area, Grace. I'm glad."

"Yes, I have. One night I saw a social media plea for funding a funeral and then another to provide for a child's future needs and then another to fund a memorial. My goodness, I got caught in the 'Help Fund Me' rabbit hole of pleas and appeals. They broke my heart. Some of the stories were compelling, and all I could think about was 'What if my family cannot write a message compelling enough to get strangers to contribute?' Just because they are not good writers does not mean they need the money any less."

"Yes, I have read them, too. Some of them make me wonder why there weren't provisions in place."

"Exactly. After learning from you, I realize how inexpensive insurance can be compared to the stress of trying to raise money when you are already going through a death, mounting bills, uncertainty, and so much more. I found myself talking to the screen. I would say things like, 'Did anyone ever talk to you about planning? Or did you ever think of getting a quote?' I know everyone doesn't have someone who explains things the way you do, but they should."

"Yes, they should. It's a tough subject, and there are a lot of people who would rather put that conversation off to another day."

"Yep, another unpromised day." Grace felt gratitude swell in her chest. "I can't thank you enough."

"It is my pleasure. Now, back to your thoughts about the first annual All-Comers meeting." She smirked at her manufactured word, and Grace giggled.

"I like that name, the Annual All-Comers meeting. I think I am going to steal it."

"Please do. It was nice watching as your advisors began to feel more comfortable adding value to one another's reports."

"They sure did. We were clear about our intention to have a productive and non-adversarial meeting. There was no room for anyone's ego and self-importance to get in the way of what we needed to accomplish. Their interactions were so productive; we thought it was a great time to look at some of the tax codes that could work in our favor, especially as we learn more about tax-free retirement income, investments, and other tax advantage options. Having my CPA, wealth manager, and insurance professional discussing what was in our best interest was exhilarating. This has never happened before!" Grace was sitting forward in the leather chair, suppressing the impulse to throw her hands up and cheer.

"Were there any other topics that stood out from the meetings?" Janise asked.

"Oh, lots! We took the time to look over our major supplier agreements to ensure they were up-to-date and accurate. It was clear to our advisors and became clearer to us that we have too much business relying on one particular customer, so we are working with our sales team to diversify our customer base. Not only is the business relying heavily on one key customer, but we are also relying too heavily on one sector, and that needs to change over time." Grace nodded, grateful that they had uncovered this.

"Another area that needed to be addressed sooner than later was employee safety in the warehouse. Getting the report alerting us to our potential workers' compensation exposure was an eye-opener. Then when our property and casualty insurance broker offered ten recommendations that would decrease our risk and increase our safety, I nearly cried. We have needed this kind of value for a long time."

"It is interesting that you included the workers' compensation report in this meeting."

"I know. We have never had a workers' compensation issue, but lately, we've had a couple of incidents that could gravely affect the bottom line. So, we thought it was important enough to be proactive and discuss it during this meeting. As you can see on the agenda, our property and casualty insurance broker attended a portion of the meeting along with our human resources representative. The brief and broad education on the importance of having safety trainings and protocols in place was invaluable."

"What did you think of the length of the meeting?"

"I think we did a good job when preparing the agenda and time allowance. We allotted the appropriate amount of time for discussions after each professional shared their report and we stuck closely to our projected timeline."

"That's fantastic. What did you learn from this experience?" Janise coaxed.

"I learned what efficiency looks like. All of the advisors who work for us should work in concert with one another. It is so much easier when they can actually hear and understand what one of the other experts is saying and doing on our behalf."

"You did a great job. There are a couple of topics that should be added to next year's annual meeting."

"Okay, what do you suggest?" Grace asked as she pulled her notepad and pen out of the purse that sat on the ground next to her.

"One thing you can talk about is how building a sellable business will be of benefit to you even if you do not plan to sell."

"That's an interesting concept. The idea of selling is not on our radar." Grace tapped the pen on her chin.

"Right, but if you and your team can work as if you do want to sell it, you're going to have a different level of intention in growing your structures and profits." Janise paused, and Grace nodded in understanding. "Also, it is good to continuously discuss your future and the plans for a smooth ownership transition. By doing this, you have now made succession planning a process and not a major or catastrophic event. It now becomes an integral part of planning for the success of your business.

"I agree. Our human resources department wants to help us create a plan for continuity, which starts at the top and trickles down into each department. We need to make sure we have crossed-trained employees."

"Yes, and we talked about having a plan in place to retain employees who are key to the success of the business. I would suggest your team clearly define what that looks like and identify who is ready for growth."

"Good idea. We still have some work to do and will certainly look at growing our staff." Just then, Grace saw people starting to file into the big double doors where the conference was beginning. "Janise, it looks like it's about to start, but I want you to know I feel like such a weight has been lifted off of my shoulders."

Janise's face lit up. "You should. Every task and item we discussed, you addressed within the timelines we set up. You had great questions and challenged your team to support the process. Now, you have a thorough succession plan. You did a great job, Grace."

Grace could feel her genuine pride from across the coffee table. "Thank you. Now, what's next?"

"Before we go, let's put our three dates on the calendar to conduct quarterly reviews. Just as in life, some circumstances and scenarios alter key performance indicators. If that is the case, we can work to restructure the tasks and goals. Also, there are a few of your colleagues here at the conference that I would love to meet. Would you mind making the introduction?"

"Are you kidding? Of course I don't mind. I have already been raving about the progress we have made in shoring up the structure of my business. In fact, several of my friends have been looking forward to meeting you at this conference."

"Thank you, Grace! And remember, I am here for you when you are ready to prepare for next year's annual meeting."

"Yes, thank you. I feel as if I have a friend for life."

Prepare to Leave In Style at:
www.LeavingInStyle.com/Resources

Conclusion
READY TO LEAVE IN STYLE?

I HOPE YOU'VE enjoyed Grace's journey and learning the basics of long-term succession planning along the way. Like you, one of the most critical roles and responsibilities that Grace has as the leader is to make decisions about the future of the company—where it goes, who are the incumbent leaders, its scalability (including timelines), and how to hedge against risks, catastrophic events, and more.

Like Grace, the actions that you take will be unique to you and your business. Her journey was designed to show you the seven significant conversations and steps that must be addressed in creating a succession plan. Still, almost all aspects of your business's succession journey will be unique and customized in most cases. After all, the business vision and mission, the services and/or products, and the staff and business dynamics you lead are like no other.

As you have seen, during the development of this plan, it is much easier when you can see the big picture and formulate a desired outcome. When a business's leadership ask for and receive support from a strategist and excellent team members, the results are more likely to lead to a sense of accomplishment, tremendous relief, and a good night's sleep for everyone involved. Plus, the business will begin to operate more efficiently toward the goals that have been set through the succession planning process.

If you could stand on the sideline and pick a team, who would you choose? What position or role would they play? How would you engage with your team? This is

the time to think about your "A-Team" and how you can
engage them as soon as possible.

> *"For executives, whose success hinges on the
> many day-to-day decisions they make or
> approve, the psychological traps
> are especially dangerous.*
>
> *They can undermine everything from new
> product development to acquisition and
> divestiture strategy to succession planning?"*
> Peter Drucker

Beware of the Traps

As a leader, let's look at a few of the most common
decision traps that may have previously stopped you from
planning and could stop you in the future if you do not
see and navigate around them.

Assumptions and Past Trends

Grace thought about her business's smooth transition
from her dad and did not realize the strategy and time
put into making a change that appeared to be seamless.
Many business owners do not take action because they
believe that the team currently in place is the one needed
to continue the business. They assume that the team will
continue to do their respective jobs, and everything will
be fine because everything has always worked out. It will
continue to work out naturally.

Procrastination

"Oh, we have plenty of time." It wasn't until Grace faced mortality with her sister's death (*and* saw the impact of her lack of planning) that she decided to stop putting off this vital decision. Tomorrow is not promised, but most business owners don't spend a lot of time imagining and preparing for unforeseen crises and disasters. They have no idea the weight they carry until they begin the planning process.

Status Quo

The idea of deciding to take action and plan for the future can be minimized by a belief that the lack of a plan won't cost the business much in time and resources. Most business owners have not experienced the unintended expenses and losses of relationships and connections. Those obligatory expenses add up quickly.

It's Time to Get Prepared to Leave in Style

I hope you have seen the many benefits of taking the time to plan for your business to continue without you and gathered some essential concepts and tools along the way.

If you get started and find you need support, please go to www.LeavingInStyle.com/Resources to explore our "Continued Conversations with Grace" as well as tools, tips, and insights that will help facilitate your process and progress.

Prepare to Leave In Style at:
www.LeavingInStyle.com/Resources

About

JANISE GRAHAM

OWNER OF ENTREPRENEUR'S Insurance Services and President of Small Business Style, Inc., Janise Graham is dedicated to small business owners and their planning needs. As a business strategist, author, coach, speaker, and trainer, Janise has made it her mission to help business owners create plans that give them a realistic perspective and peace of mind. Her results-focused process helps them recognize and reach milestones that lead to successful outcomes. She has advised, coached, and counseled more than 500 business owners and entrepreneurs in various phases of their business.

More than twenty years ago, after working for two of the nation's largest insurance companies, Janise became a business owner to serve other business owners. After seeing what can happen to a very successful enterprise when there is no business succession plan, Janise was compelled to redirect her abilities to make the complexities of planning more palatable for the small business owner.

Her mission and passion are to help business owners and executives understand the importance of a business succession plan and implement one to help their businesses and families continue to thrive beyond a significant loss or disability.

As an industry leader, she is the Past President of the National Association of Women Business Owners (NAWBO)-Inland Empire and a NAWBO Presidents Assembly Steering Committee member, and serves on the California Board for the National Association of Insurance and Financial Advisors (NAIFA) and AmPac Business Capital. She has served two terms as President of NAIFA Inland Empire, is a past President of Business Resource Connection, and is currently a member of Life Enhancing Advisors (LEA).

Janise holds a Bachelor of Arts degree in Business Administration from California Baptist University, a Fashion Merchandising Business Degree from Brooks College, and a Certification in Executive Women in Leadership from Cornell University. She is a Leadership In Life Institute graduate, certified in Long Term Care (CLTC), and is a Life and Annuity Certified Professional (LACP).

Janise lives in Southern California with her husband, Larry. She is the proud mom of three daughters and has three adorable grandsons.

A Special
INVITATION

"The best way to predict the
future is to create it."
Peter Drucker

MY INTENTION FOR this book was to create awareness and encourage you to envision and design your own destiny. Now that Grace has inspired you to get started, I want to help you keep that momentum and take time to strategize and explore your options.

At www.LeavingInStyle.com/Resources, you will find a repository of tools based on the conversations you witnessed in this story which include:

- an assessment to gauge your exit readiness
- actionable worksheets to help you organizes your thoughts and processes
- tips and ideas for getting the most out of your professional team and enhancing the structure of your successful business
- an invitation to join our masterclass and discover more of what it takes to Leave In Style

**If you want more, consider joining
one of our programs.**

Active enrollment in one of our program(s) will give you access to Monthly Q &A calls. These conversations are a safe space for tough questions and concerns about business systems, organizational structure, performance improvement, developing a plan, and more.

LOOKING FORWARD
TO HELPING YOU

Leave In Style!

Supporting
WOMEN IN BUSINESS

HAVE YOU EVER had one of those moments in business when you met someone and instantly knew there was a connection? Fortunately, I have had that experience several times. One such instance was in 2003 when my business coach, the late Ruben Estrada, was speaking at an event and invited me to attend. Ruben was the best at making warm introductions; he would give so much detail about the individuals he was connecting that you could not help but want to engage and get to know the other person better.

In this instance, the warm, energetic, and engaging lady that he connected me with was Michelle Skiljan, Executive Director of the newly opened women's business center in our community.

As we spoke, I learned more about Michelle's mission and desire to bring quality content, workshops, conferences, and professional resources to all of the women in the Inland Empire. I was so excited about the prospect of being in service, I asked if I could teach a class that would help women better understand how to manage their finances and mitigate risks. She agreed and that was the beginning of our personal and business relationship, which has spanned almost two decades.

The Inland Empire Women's Business Center (IEWBC) has actively reached out to lift thousands of low-to-moderate-income women from a vision or a dream to empowerment with the knowledge and capacity to become an entrepreneur. Of course, there were also women with proven business success who could also count on the much-needed support as they scaled their businesses to new heights.

The Inland Empire Women's Business Center is a program of the Inland Empire Center of Entrepreneurship (IECE) at California State University San Bernardino and is partially funded by the U.S. Small Business Administration (SBA). The SBA requires that the funding provided to the center be matched by way of other grants and donations.

It is because of Michelle's tremendous dedication and support for women, not only in our community but across the country, that I will donate a portion of the profits from this book to the Inland Empire Women's Business Center and other women in business causes and centers across the nation.

Thank you, Michelle, for being the most incredible intrapreneur, a tremendous supporter, a light in the community, and most importantly, a friend.

To learn more about and to support the Inland Empire Women's Business Center, go to www.IEWBC.org

To learn more about Women's Business Centers across the United States, go to the www.AWBC.org/wbc-locator/

ACKNOWLEDGMENTS

MY WORLD IS so full of kind and loving people. It would require a chapter to include them all.

My Family

To my husband Larry, you have always reminded me to put one foot in front of the other and keep moving. You have never complained about my multiple full-time activities and have given me the space needed to write and rewrite this body of work. We are a team and have come a long way. I love you.

To my children, Lauren (and Bho), Alchemy, and Alanna, I am blessed beyond measure to have such brilliant, beautiful, and amazing young adults who exude honesty, love, and light. It is an honor to watch and learn from you. To my grandsons Darian, Liam, and Greyson, you make my heart flutter.

To my mom, you were my first role model in both fashion as a designer and runway model and in business as a sales rep for a fortune 500 company. Your simple and literal swimming instruction "When you think you are drowning, wait 'til you get out of the water to panic" are words of wisdom that I live by. They have served me well.

To my siblings. Tammi, thank you for your amazing support always and throughout this book writing process. You have an impeccable eye, thought-provoking questions, and a true care and concern. Marques, no words can express how proud I am of you and where your

life's journey has brought you. Your quest for growth
and knowledge is commendable. Thank you both for
always being a reminder of unconditional love. To my
nephew, Kalin Phillips, the future entrepreneur. A part of
a successful strategy is to begin with the end in mind.

My Pride

I admire the lionesses and their pride as they rear their
cubs, work (hunt), play, and fight together. There is no
hierarchy but a community of unity and collaboration.
This is how I see my sister-friends. They are a part of
my Pride.

To my twin, Ursula Mentjes. Without you, I would
not have been on this book journey. Your persistent
yet gentle pushes to share what I know with the world
was the kind of love and support I needed. Thank you.
Jacqueline Brinson-Ederaine, our sisterhood has spanned
more than thirty years. Thank you for being such a warm
and loving supporter. Cecilia (C.C.) Vest, besides being ·
there when I needed you most, you are truly a beacon
and inspiration to those who want to "Leave In Style."
LaVonne Shields, you are a great accountability partner
and are a good source of free entertainment! (Where are
the cameras?) Michelle Skiljan, you have been a lifeline
and a safety net. I can't thank you enough for being the
light during good times and tough times. Tracy Bennett
and Donna English, you were both by my side, pulling
me towards the action and insisting that I remain social
when it would have been so easy to sit in the dark. When
is our next adventure?

My Colleagues

The National Association of Insurance and Financial Advisors consist of an incredible group of professionals. Many have been a shining example of what is possible. Although there are too many to name, there are a few who must be recognized. John Davidson, you were the first person to see in me what I did not see. Thank you for the awakening. Mike Ables, your support and friendship means the world to me. Dawn Coleman, your passion and conviction are contagious. Peter Buechler, Marc Bregman, and Denise Boyce Bustamente, when I think of you, I smile because you have made this journey fun, fun, fun!

My Team

To Amanda Johnson and the True To Intention team, if only you could edit the rest of my world. Amanda, thank you so much for being such an amazing guide for me in these uncharted waters. Your encouragement and emails cheering "we're almost there" kept me focused and pushing forward. Dan Mulhern, working with you over the past decade has always been a joy. You are such a good listener and convert ramblings into magic. Saima Latif, this may be the first time your fashion illustrations are used in a business book. Thank you for being so easy to work with. Thank you, Jebe Jamorol, my assistant who is always willing to jump in and help where needed.

My Community

To my Business Resource Connection sisters—Debra
Murphy, Palbinder Badesha, Wanda Wilson, Dian
Wyman, Sophia Brooks, Lynn Hounsley-Michalski,
Nicole Kinney, Marcy Decato, and GiGi Mindreau-
Banks—thank you for helping me work through my
chapters and online course. A special thank you to Dian
Wyman for your wisdom, advice, and insight.

To The Crew, Debra McDaniel's, Leah Brown, Kietta
Surratt, and Veronica Brooks, your daily text of greetings
and inspiration are a welcome respite.

To Life Enhancing Advisors and especially Emily
Prendiville, you have opened up a new world of personal
growth which is giving me clarity and life balance.

To my NAWBO sisters across the U.S., it is an
honor to walk beside you as we advocate for women in
business.

To Fierce Book Club, you were my introduction into
the world of fiction. Without you, I am not sure if I could
have vividly expressed Grace's voice.

Thank you, John Anderson, Joe Atchison, Rick
Bisio, and Lynn Shelton, for being so generous with
your knowledge and expertise as I embarked on the
original iteration of Leaving In Style. A special Thank
you to Denise Jurina Nelson, for sharing your story and
the circumstances that changed your life in February
2001. Your personal tragedy awakened my curiosity and
changed the trajectory of my business.

My Muse

To Janet (Jan) Steiner, who I affectionately call my business celebrity. Your willingness to share your wisdom with other women business owners, and your heart for philanthropy, only makes me admire you more. Your journey and story have truly been an inspiration to me. You are also the epitome of Leaving In Style! Thank you so much for being such a tremendous support to me and my desire to make a difference.

To all of the readers who previewed this book, thank you for your time and your feedback. This book is more true to me and more powerful because of you.

With All My Love and Gratitude,

Janai Graham